Publisher: SW Ventures LLC.
ISBN: 979-8333844637
First Edition: July 2024

Printed in the United States of America.

AI AGENTS

EVERYTHING YOU NEED TO KNOW

A Comprehensive Guide to Understanding and Implementing AI Agents

FIRST EDITION

Sunny Wu

Author's Note

Artificial Intelligence (AI) has significantly advanced in the past two years, primarily driven by the evolution of Large Language Models (LLM) and Neural Networks. With the popularity of applications like ChatGPT and Tesla's Full Self-Driving (FSD) system, AI has seamlessly integrated into our daily lives, transitioning from a mere concept to a tangible reality.

In this new wave of AI, AI Agents have emerged as a crucial concept, framework, and application that connects us with AI. These agents mimic human cognitive functions such as learning, reasoning, and problem-solving, enabling them to perform complex tasks with minimal human intervention. As AI agents become more prevalent, understanding their concepts, capabilities, benefits, and implications is crucial for both individuals and businesses. This book aims to demystify AI agents, providing a comprehensive guide to their role in our present and future.

Empowering both businesses and individuals, this book offers practical insights and strategies for integrating AI into various operations. Navigating the AI landscape can be complex and rapidly evolving. This book also serves as a roadmap, guiding you through the myriad of AI technologies, trends, and best practices. From foundational concepts to applications, you will gain a solid understanding of what AI agents are and how they can be utilized effectively.

With the rise of AI come important ethical and practical considerations. Issues such as privacy, data security, job implications, and workforce changes are addressed, providing a balanced perspective on the benefits and challenges of AI agents.

This book tackles these critical questions head-on, helping you understand and manage the risks associated with AI.

As a serial entrepreneur, I have dedicated my career to productizing and commercializing AI agents for years, across both the education and smart home industries. My two-decade-long journey in technology has been driven by a passion for innovation and a deep understanding of how AI can transform both business and personal life. My experience in integrating AI technologies into consumer products has provided me with unique insights into the practical applications and strategic benefits of AI agents. I have witnessed firsthand how AI can drive business growth, enhance customer satisfaction, and create new opportunities for innovation.

In this book, I aim to share these observations and insights with you, offering a comprehensive guide to understanding, implementing, and leveraging AI agents. Whether you are a business leader, an entrepreneur, or someone simply curious about the future of AI, I hope this book will equip you with the knowledge and tools to navigate the AI landscape confidently.

Sunny Wu

May 2024 @ Seattle

CONTENTS

Chapter 1: Welcome to the World of AI Agents

The Rise of AI in Everyday Life

Imagine waking up in the morning to the gentle sound of your favorite music, as your AI-powered assistant gradually adjusts the lights to simulate a natural sunrise. Your coffee maker, connected to the same AI system, begins brewing your favorite blend just in time for you to step into the kitchen. As you enjoy your coffee, your virtual assistant updates you on the weather, your schedule, and the latest news, all tailored to your interests and preferences.

This is not a scene from a science fiction movie anymore; it is the reality of AI in our everyday lives. Artificial Intelligence (AI) has rapidly evolved from a niche technology into a ubiquitous presence that permeates nearly every aspect of our daily routines. From smart home devices like Wyze Cameras, and personal assistants like Amazon's Alexa and Google Assistant to sophisticated recommendation systems on Netflix and Spotify, AI agents are transforming how we interact with the world around us.

The integration of AI into everyday life is driven by advancements in neural network, machine learning, natural language processing, and data analytics. These technologies enable AI models and AI agents to understand, learn from, and respond to human behavior in increasingly sophisticated ways. Whether it's automating mundane tasks, providing personalized recommendations, or even driving cars, AI agents are designed to enhance efficiency, convenience, and overall quality of life.

In businesses, AI agents are revolutionizing industries by optimizing operations, improving customer service, and driving innovation. Companies leverage AI to gain insights from vast amounts of data, predict market trends, and create more engaging customer experiences. The potential applications of AI agents are vast, and their impact is profound, reshaping the landscape of both personal and professional environments.

The Evolution of AI Technology

The journey of AI from a theoretical concept to a practical reality has been nothing short of remarkable. Early AI research focused on symbolic reasoning and rule-based systems, where computers were programmed with explicit instructions to perform specific tasks. These early systems were limited by their inability to adapt or learn from new information, making them brittle and inflexible.

The advent of machine learning marked a significant turning point in AI development. Instead of relying on pre-defined rules, machine learning algorithms enable computers to learn patterns and make decisions based on data. This shift allowed AI systems to become more adaptable and capable of handling complex, real-world tasks.

Deep learning, a subset of machine learning, has further propelled AI's capabilities. By utilizing neural networks with multiple layers, deep learning models can automatically learn hierarchical representations of data, leading to breakthroughs in image and speech recognition, natural language processing, and more. The combination of increased computational power and vast amounts of data has enabled deep learning models to achieve unprecedented levels of accuracy and performance.

Everyday Interactions with AI Agents

AI agents have seamlessly integrated into various aspects of our daily lives, often in ways we may not even realize. Here are a few examples of how AI agents are enhancing our everyday experiences:

Smart Home Devices: AI-powered devices like smart speakers, thermostats, and security cameras have become common fixtures in modern homes. These devices can control lighting, adjust temperature settings, monitor security, and even provide voice-activated assistance, creating a more comfortable and secure living environment.

Personal Assistants: Virtual assistants such as Siri, Google Assistant, and Alexa have become indispensable tools for managing daily tasks. They can set reminders, send messages, answer questions, and provide personalized recommendations based on user preferences and habits.

Entertainment and Media: AI-driven recommendation systems on platforms like Netflix, Spotify, and YouTube curate content tailored to individual tastes, ensuring a more engaging and enjoyable user experience. These systems analyze viewing and listening habits to suggest movies, TV shows, music, and videos that align with user preferences.

Healthcare and Wellness: AI agents are playing a growing role in healthcare, from diagnosing medical conditions to providing personalized wellness recommendations. Wearable devices and health apps use AI to track physical activity, monitor vital signs, and offer insights into overall health and well-being.

Transportation: Autonomous vehicles and AI-assisted navigation systems are transforming the way we travel. Self-driving cars, powered by advanced AI algorithms, promise to improve road safety, reduce traffic congestion, and provide greater accessibility to transportation.

Communication: AI-powered chatbots and customer support agents are enhancing communication by providing instant, accurate responses to queries. These AI agents can handle a wide range of tasks, from answering frequently asked questions to assisting with complex problem-solving.

The Business Transformation Driven by AI

AI agents are not only enhancing our personal lives but also driving significant transformations in the business world. Companies across various industries are leveraging AI to streamline operations, improve customer experiences, and drive innovation. Here are a few ways AI agents are making an impact:

Customer Service: AI-powered chatbots and virtual assistants are revolutionizing customer service by providing instant support and resolving issues efficiently. These AI agents can handle a wide range of customer queries, freeing up human agents to focus on more complex tasks.

Marketing and Sales: AI-driven analytics tools are enabling businesses to gain deeper insights into customer behavior and preferences. By analyzing data from various sources, AI agents can identify patterns, predict trends, and provide personalized recommendations, leading to more effective marketing campaigns and increased sales.

Supply Chain Management: AI agents are optimizing supply chain operations by predicting demand, managing inventory, and identifying potential disruptions. These capabilities help businesses reduce costs, improve efficiency, and ensure timely delivery of products and services.

Financial Services: AI is transforming the financial industry by automating processes, detecting fraud, and providing personalized financial advice. AI agents can analyze large volumes of financial data to identify risks, make investment recommendations, and streamline compliance processes.

Healthcare: In the healthcare sector, AI agents are assisting in diagnostics, treatment planning, and patient care. AI-driven tools can analyze medical images, predict disease progression, and provide personalized treatment recommendations, improving patient outcomes and reducing healthcare costs.

Manufacturing: AI-powered automation and predictive maintenance are enhancing manufacturing processes. AI agents can monitor equipment performance, predict failures, and optimize production schedules, leading to increased efficiency and reduced downtime.

The Potential and Promise of AI Agents

The potential applications of AI agents are vast and continually expanding as technology advances. Here are a few areas where AI agents are poised to make significant contributions:

Education: AI agents have the potential to revolutionize education by providing personalized learning experiences. Intelligent tutoring systems can adapt to individual learning styles, offering customized lessons and feedback to help students achieve their full potential.

Environmental Sustainability: AI agents can play a critical role in addressing environmental challenges. From optimizing energy usage in smart grids to monitoring and mitigating the impact of climate change, AI-driven solutions can help create a more sustainable future.

Agriculture: AI agents are transforming agriculture by enabling precision farming techniques. AI-powered tools can analyze soil conditions, monitor crop health, and optimize irrigation and fertilization, leading to increased yields and reduced resource consumption.

Public Safety: AI agents are enhancing public safety through applications such as predictive policing, disaster response, and cybersecurity. By analyzing data and identifying potential threats,

AI-driven systems can help prevent and mitigate risks to public safety.

Humanitarian Aid: AI agents are being used to improve humanitarian aid efforts by optimizing resource allocation, predicting crisis hotspots, and providing real-time insights into disaster response. These capabilities can help organizations deliver aid more effectively and efficiently.

The Ethical and Societal Implications of AI

As AI agents become more integrated into our lives, it is essential to consider the ethical and societal implications of their use. Here are a few key considerations:

Privacy and Data Security: The widespread use of AI agents raises concerns about privacy and data security. Ensuring that personal data is protected and used ethically is critical to maintaining public trust in AI technologies.

Bias and Fairness: AI systems can inadvertently perpetuate biases present in the data they are trained on. It is essential to develop and implement strategies to ensure that AI agents are fair and unbiased in their decision-making processes.

Job Displacement: The automation of tasks by AI agents has the potential to displace certain jobs, leading to economic and social challenges. It is important to consider strategies for workforce retraining and support to help individuals adapt to the changing job landscape.

Accountability and Transparency: As AI agents make decisions that impact people's lives, it is crucial to ensure that these systems are transparent and accountable. Clear guidelines and regulations are needed to govern the development and deployment of AI technologies.

Ethical Use of AI: Establishing ethical guidelines for the use of AI is essential to ensure that these technologies are developed and used in ways that benefit society. This includes considering the long-term implications of AI and prioritizing human well-being.

Looking Ahead

In the chapters that follow, we will delve deeper into the world of AI agents, exploring their technical foundations, business applications, and personal impacts. We will uncover the transformative power of AI, providing you with the insights and guidance needed to embrace this technology confidently and responsibly.

Welcome to the world of AI agents – a world of endless possibilities and exciting opportunities.

Chapter 2: What Are AI Agents?

Definitions and Concepts

The Basics of AI Agents

Artificial Intelligence (AI) agents are software entities designed to perform tasks autonomously or semi-autonomously, using data to make decisions and improve over time. At their core, AI agents mimic human cognitive functions such as learning, reasoning, and problem-solving, enabling them to carry out complex tasks with minimal human intervention. These agents can range from simple rule-based systems to sophisticated entities capable of understanding natural language, recognizing patterns, and making predictions.

The term "agent" in AI refers to an entity that can perceive its environment through sensors and act upon that environment using actuators. In the context of software, these sensors and actuators are typically digital inputs and outputs, such as data from a database or responses to user queries. The intelligence of the agent comes from its ability to process this data, learn from it, and make informed decisions or recommendations.

Key Characteristics of AI Agents

AI agents possess several key characteristics that differentiate them from traditional software programs:

Autonomy: AI agents operate without direct human control, making decisions based on their programming and the data they process. This autonomy allows them to perform tasks continuously and efficiently.

Reactivity: AI agents can perceive changes in their environment and respond appropriately. This reactivity enables them to adapt to new information and dynamic conditions, ensuring their actions remain relevant and effective.

Proactivity: Beyond merely reacting to changes, AI agents can take initiative. They can plan and execute actions to achieve specific goals, often anticipating needs and opportunities before they arise.

Social Ability: Many AI agents are designed to interact with humans or other agents. This social ability includes understanding natural language, recognizing emotions, and engaging in meaningful conversations or collaborations.

Historical Context

The Foundations of AI

The concept of artificial intelligence has roots that extend far back into history, long before the advent of modern computers. Philosophers and visionaries have long speculated about the possibility of creating machines that could emulate human intelligence. However, the formal foundation of AI as a scientific discipline was established in the mid-20th century. This section delves into the pivotal moments and key figures that laid the groundwork for the development of AI.

Early Philosophical Foundations

The idea of intelligent machines can be traced back to ancient civilizations. The Greeks, for example, had myths about automatons created by the gods. However, it wasn't until the Age of Enlightenment that more concrete ideas began to form. In the 17th century, French philosopher René Descartes proposed the concept of mechanistic philosophy, suggesting that human and animal bodies operate like machines. This idea paved the way for thinking about the mind as a machine that could potentially be replicated.

In the 18th century, mathematician and philosopher Gottfried Wilhelm Leibniz dreamt of creating a universal language of logic, a precursor to the binary code that underpins modern computing.

Leibniz's work on logic and binary arithmetic laid essential groundwork for future developments in both computer science and AI.

The Birth of Computing: Alan Turing and the Turing Machine

A significant milestone in the foundations of AI was the work of British mathematician Alan Turing. In 1936, Turing introduced the concept of the Turing machine, a theoretical device that could simulate the logic of any computer algorithm. This abstract machine became a cornerstone of computer science, demonstrating that a machine could perform any computation that could be described algorithmically.

Turing's work went beyond theoretical constructs. During World War II, he played a crucial role in breaking the Enigma code used by the Germans, demonstrating the practical applications of computational machines. After the war, Turing continued to explore the possibilities of machine intelligence. In 1950, he published a seminal paper titled "Computing Machinery and Intelligence," in which he proposed the famous Turing Test to determine whether a machine could exhibit intelligent behavior indistinguishable from that of a human.

The Dartmouth Conference and the Birth of AI

The formal establishment of AI as a field of study occurred in 1956 during the Dartmouth Conference. Organized by John McCarthy, Marvin Minsky, Nathaniel Rochester, and Claude Shannon, the conference brought together leading researchers to discuss the possibilities of creating machines that could think. The proposal for the conference included the bold claim that "every aspect of learning or any other feature of intelligence can in principle be so precisely described that a machine can be made to simulate it."

This conference is often considered the birthplace of AI as an academic discipline. It led to the coining of the term "artificial intelligence" and sparked a wave of optimism and funding for AI research. The participants envisioned creating machines that could perform tasks requiring human intelligence, such as reasoning, learning, and understanding natural language.

Early AI Programs and Symbolic AI

Following the Dartmouth Conference, the 1950s and 1960s saw the development of several pioneering AI programs. These early efforts were primarily based on symbolic AI, which relied on manipulating symbols and applying rules to simulate human intelligence. Some notable early AI programs include:

Logic Theorist: Developed by Allen Newell and Herbert A. Simon in 1955, Logic Theorist was one of the first AI programs. It was designed to prove mathematical theorems by representing problems as formal logic statements and using rules to manipulate these statements. Logic Theorist successfully proved several theorems from Principia Mathematica, a landmark work in mathematical logic.

General Problem Solver (GPS): Also developed by Newell and Simon, GPS was a more ambitious project aimed at solving a wide range of problems. GPS used heuristics, or "rules of thumb," to guide its search for solutions. While it achieved some success, GPS struggled with more complex problems due to the limitations of computational power and the complexity of real-world scenarios.

ELIZA: Created by Joseph Weizenbaum in the mid-1960s, ELIZA was an early natural language processing program that could simulate conversation with a human. ELIZA used simple pattern matching and substitution to respond to user inputs, creating the illusion of understanding. Although limited in its capabilities,

ELIZA demonstrated the potential for AI to interact with humans through natural language.

The AI Boom and Initial Optimism

The success of early AI programs generated significant optimism and funding for AI research. Governments, universities, and private companies invested heavily in AI projects, believing that machines capable of human-like intelligence were just around the corner. Researchers focused on developing rule-based systems, or expert systems, that could emulate the decision-making processes of human experts in specific domains.

Challenges and Setbacks: The AI Winter

Despite the initial enthusiasm, the limitations of symbolic AI became increasingly apparent. Rule-based systems struggled with the complexity and variability of real-world environments. They were brittle, unable to adapt to new situations or learn from experience. As a result, many ambitious AI projects failed to deliver on their promises, leading to a decline in funding and interest in AI research. This period of reduced funding and interest is known as the "AI Winter."

The first AI winter occurred in the 1970s, as the limitations of early AI approaches became clear. The second AI winter in the late 1980s and early 1990s resulted from the collapse of the market for expert systems and other rule-based AI technologies. During these periods, many researchers shifted their focus to other areas, and AI research entered a phase of stagnation.

The Resurgence: Machine Learning and Neural Networks

The resurgence of AI began in the 1990s with the advent of machine learning, a paradigm shift that emphasized learning from data rather than relying solely on predefined rules. Machine learning algorithms enabled AI systems to identify patterns, make predictions, and improve over time. This approach proved to be more flexible and scalable, leading to significant advancements in various AI applications.

A key milestone in this resurgence was the development of artificial neural networks, inspired by the structure and function of the human brain. These networks, composed of interconnected nodes (neurons), allowed AI agents to process and learn from vast amounts of data. This breakthrough paved the way for more advanced AI applications, including image and speech recognition.

The revival of interest in neural networks was significantly boosted by advancements in computational power and the availability of large datasets. Researchers like Geoffrey Hinton, Yann LeCun, and Yoshua Bengio made pioneering contributions to the field of deep learning, which involves training neural networks with multiple layers to learn hierarchical representations of data. Their work laid the foundation for many of the AI breakthroughs we see today.

Deep Learning: A Revolution in AI

Deep learning has been a game-changer in the field of AI. Unlike traditional machine learning algorithms that require manual feature extraction, deep learning models can automatically learn features from raw data. This capability has led to significant improvements in performance across a wide range of tasks.

1. **Convolutional Neural Networks (CNNs)**: CNNs are a type of deep learning model specifically designed for processing grid-like data, such as images. They use convolutional layers to automatically detect features like edges, textures, and shapes, making them highly effective for image classification, object detection, and other computer vision tasks.
2. **Recurrent Neural Networks (RNNs)**: RNNs are designed for sequential data, such as time series or natural language. They maintain a hidden state that captures information about previous inputs, allowing them to model dependencies over time. Variants like Long Short-Term Memory (LSTM) networks and Gated Recurrent Units (GRUs) have further improved the ability of RNNs to handle long-term dependencies.
3. **Transformer Models**: Transformers, introduced by Vaswani et al. in 2017, have revolutionized natural language processing. Unlike RNNs, transformers use self-attention mechanisms to process input sequences in parallel, making them highly efficient and effective. Transformer-based models like GEMINI, GPT-4, and T5 have set new benchmarks in tasks such as language translation, text generation, and question answering.

The Role of Big Data and GPUs

The success of deep learning has been fueled by the availability of large datasets and powerful computational resources. The rise of the internet and digitalization has generated vast amounts of data, providing the fuel for training deep learning models. Additionally, Graphics Processing Units (GPUs), originally designed for rendering graphics in video games, have proven to be highly effective for the parallel processing required by deep learning algorithms.

Companies like NVIDIA have developed specialized hardware and software frameworks that make it easier to train and deploy deep learning models at scale. Cloud computing platforms from providers like Amazon Web Services (AWS), Google Cloud, and Microsoft Azure have further democratized access to the computational resources needed for AI research and development.

The Impact of Deep Learning on AI Applications

Deep learning has transformed numerous fields and applications, demonstrating the versatility and power of AI. Some notable examples include:

1. **Computer Vision**: Deep learning models have achieved human-level performance in image classification tasks and have been applied to facial recognition, autonomous driving, medical image analysis, and more. Companies like Tesla, Google, and Facebook leverage computer vision technologies to develop innovative products and services.
2. **Natural Language Processing**: Transformer-based models have enabled significant advancements in language understanding and generation. AI agents can now perform tasks such as language translation, sentiment analysis, text summarization, and conversational AI with remarkable accuracy. Virtual assistants like Google Assistant, Siri, and Alexa rely on these models to provide intelligent and natural interactions.
3. **Healthcare**: Deep learning models are being used to analyze medical images, predict disease outcomes, and personalize treatment plans. AI agents assist radiologists in detecting anomalies in X-rays and MRIs, and they help researchers identify potential drug candidates by analyzing biological data.
4. **Gaming and Entertainment**: AI agents powered by deep learning have achieved superhuman performance in

complex games like Go, Dota 2, and StarCraft II. These achievements not only showcase the capabilities of AI but also provide valuable insights into strategic decision-making and planning.

5. **Autonomous Systems**: Deep learning is a critical component of autonomous vehicles, enabling them to perceive their environment, make decisions, and navigate safely. Companies like Waymo, Uber, and Tesla are at the forefront of developing self-driving cars that leverage AI for real-time perception and control.

Differentiating AI Agents from General AI

Narrow AI vs. General AI

When discussing AI agents, it is essential to differentiate between narrow AI and general AI. Narrow AI, also known as weak AI, refers to systems designed to perform specific tasks within a limited domain. These agents excel at tasks like image recognition, language translation, or recommendation systems, but they do not possess the broad cognitive abilities of a human being.

In contrast, general AI, also known as strong AI or artificial general intelligence (AGI), refers to systems with the ability to understand, learn, and apply knowledge across a wide range of tasks, similar to human intelligence. AGI remains a theoretical concept, as current AI agents are specialized and lack the versatility and adaptability of human cognition.

Practical Applications of Narrow AI Agents

Most AI agents in use today fall under the category of narrow AI. These agents are highly effective at performing specific tasks and are widely deployed across various industries. Some practical applications of narrow AI agents include:

Customer Support: AI-powered chatbots and virtual assistants handle customer inquiries, provide information, and resolve issues, improving efficiency and customer satisfaction.

Healthcare: AI agents assist in diagnosing medical conditions, predicting patient outcomes, and personalizing treatment plans, enhancing the quality of care.

Finance: AI-driven algorithms analyze market trends, detect fraudulent activities, and provide personalized financial advice, optimizing financial operations and security.

Retail: Recommendation systems powered by AI suggest products to customers based on their preferences and purchase history, boosting sales and customer engagement.

Transportation: Autonomous vehicles and AI-enhanced traffic management systems improve safety, reduce congestion, and enhance overall transportation efficiency.

The Ongoing Quest for General AI

While narrow AI agents have achieved remarkable success, the pursuit of general AI remains a significant challenge. Researchers are exploring various approaches to develop AGI, including enhancing machine learning algorithms, advancing neural network architectures, and integrating cognitive science insights.

The journey toward AGI involves addressing complex issues such as common-sense reasoning, transfer learning (the ability to apply knowledge from one domain to another), and achieving human-like understanding and empathy. Despite these challenges, the pursuit of AGI continues to drive innovation and inspire new breakthroughs in AI research.

The Building Blocks of AI Agents

Machine Learning and Neural Networks

Machine learning is the foundation of many AI agents, enabling them to learn from data and improve over time. Machine learning algorithms can be broadly categorized into three types: supervised learning, unsupervised learning, and reinforcement learning.

Supervised Learning: In supervised learning, AI agents are trained on labeled data, where each input has a corresponding output. The agent learns to map inputs to outputs by minimizing the difference between its predictions and the actual labels. Common applications include image classification, language translation, and spam detection.

Unsupervised Learning: Unsupervised learning involves training AI agents on unlabeled data, where the agent must identify patterns and structures without explicit guidance. Clustering and dimensionality reduction are common techniques used in unsupervised learning, with applications in anomaly detection, market segmentation, and data visualization.

Reinforcement Learning: In reinforcement learning, AI agents learn by interacting with an environment and receiving feedback in the form of rewards or penalties. The agent aims to maximize cumulative rewards by learning optimal actions through trial and error. Reinforcement learning is widely used in robotics, game playing, and autonomous systems.

Neural networks, inspired by the human brain's structure, are a crucial component of many machine learning models. These networks consist of interconnected nodes (neurons) organized into layers. The layers process and transform data, enabling the network to learn complex patterns and representations. Deep learning, which involves neural networks with multiple layers, has been instrumental in achieving state-of-the-art performance in various AI applications.

Natural Language Processing

Natural Language Processing (NLP) is a field of AI focused on enabling machines to understand, interpret, and generate human language. NLP techniques are essential for creating AI agents that can interact with humans through text or speech. Key components of NLP include:

Text Analysis: Techniques such as tokenization, stemming, and lemmatization break down text into manageable units and normalize them for analysis. This preprocessing is crucial for understanding the structure and meaning of text.

Sentiment Analysis: AI agents can analyze text to determine the sentiment or emotion expressed by the writer. Sentiment analysis is widely used in social media monitoring, customer feedback analysis, and market research.

Language Generation: AI agents can generate human-like text, enabling applications such as chatbots, content creation, and translation. Techniques like recurrent neural networks (RNNs) and transformer models (e.g., GPT-4) have significantly advanced language generation capabilities.

Speech Recognition and Synthesis: NLP also encompasses converting spoken language into text (speech recognition) and generating spoken language from text (speech synthesis). These technologies enable voice-activated assistants, transcription services, and accessible communication tools.

Computer Vision

Computer vision is a field of AI that enables machines to interpret and understand visual information from the world. AI agents equipped with computer vision capabilities can analyze images and videos, enabling applications such as:

Object Detection: Identifying and locating objects within an image or video frame. This technology is used in autonomous vehicles, security systems, and medical imaging.

Image Classification: Categorizing images into predefined classes based on their content. Image classification is used in applications like facial recognition, scene analysis, and content filtering.

Image Segmentation: Dividing an image into distinct regions based on the objects or structures present. Image segmentation is crucial for applications such as medical image analysis, autonomous driving, and augmented reality.

Visual Recognition: Recognizing and understanding the content of images and videos. Visual recognition is used in applications like surveillance, robotics, and consumer electronics.

Automation and Robotics

AI agents are at the forefront of automation and robotics, enabling machines to perform tasks traditionally done by humans. These agents can control robots, manage processes, and optimize operations across various industries. Key areas of automation and robotics include:

Industrial Automation: AI agents control manufacturing processes, optimize production lines, and ensure quality control. This automation improves efficiency, reduces costs, and enhances product quality.

Robotic Process Automation (RPA): RPA involves using AI agents to automate repetitive tasks in business processes, such as data entry, invoice processing, and customer support. RPA improves productivity and accuracy while freeing up human workers for more strategic tasks.

Service Robotics: AI-powered robots assist in healthcare, hospitality, and retail environments. These robots can perform tasks such as patient care, cleaning, and inventory management, improving service quality and efficiency.

Autonomous Systems: AI agents enable autonomous vehicles, drones, and other systems to navigate and operate independently.

These technologies have applications in transportation, logistics, agriculture, and defense.

Social and Collaborative Agents

AI agents with social and collaborative abilities are designed to interact with humans and other agents in meaningful ways. These agents can understand and respond to human emotions, collaborate on tasks, and provide companionship. Key aspects of social and collaborative agents include:

Emotion Recognition: AI agents can analyze facial expressions, voice tones, and text to identify human emotions. This capability enables more empathetic and responsive interactions in applications such as customer support, mental health care, and education.

Natural Language Interaction: Social agents can engage in natural language conversations, understanding context and providing relevant responses. This interaction is essential for virtual assistants, chatbots, and social robots.

Collaboration and Teamwork: AI agents can work alongside humans and other agents to achieve common goals. Collaborative agents are used in environments like smart offices, where they assist with scheduling, project management, and information sharing.

Companionship and Support: AI agents can provide companionship and support to individuals, particularly in settings such as elder care, mental health, and education. These agents offer personalized interactions and help alleviate loneliness and stress.

The Future of AI Agents

The field of AI agents is continually evolving, with new advancements and applications emerging regularly. Here are a few areas where AI agents are expected to make significant strides in the coming years:

Enhanced Personalization: AI agents will become even more adept at understanding individual preferences and needs, offering highly personalized experiences in areas such as healthcare, education, and entertainment.

Improved Human-AI Collaboration: The integration of AI agents into the workplace will enhance collaboration between humans and machines, leading to increased productivity, creativity, and innovation.

Advanced Autonomous Systems: The development of more sophisticated autonomous systems will revolutionize industries such as transportation, logistics, and agriculture, improving efficiency and sustainability.

AI for Social Good: AI agents will play a crucial role in addressing global challenges such as climate change, healthcare disparities, and education access. These agents will provide innovative solutions and insights to drive positive social impact.

Ethical and Responsible AI: The focus on ethical AI development will ensure that AI agents are designed and deployed in ways that prioritize fairness, transparency, and accountability. This approach will build trust and mitigate potential risks associated with AI technologies.

Summary

In this chapter, we have explored the fundamental concepts of AI agents, their historical development, and their key characteristics. We have also examined the various types of AI agents and their applications across different domains. Understanding what AI agents are and how they operate is the first step in harnessing their potential to transform our lives and businesses.

As we delve deeper into the world of AI agents in the following chapters, we will explore their technical foundations, business applications, and personal impacts in greater detail. By gaining a comprehensive understanding of AI agents, you will be better equipped to navigate the AI landscape and leverage these powerful tools to achieve your goals.

Chapter 3: How AI Agents Work

Core Technologies Behind AI Agents

To understand how AI agents work, it's essential to explore the core technologies that power them. These technologies include machine learning, neural networks, natural language processing, and automation systems. Each of these technologies contributes to the ability of AI agents to learn, adapt, and perform tasks autonomously.

Machine Learning

Machine learning (ML) is a subset of artificial intelligence that focuses on developing algorithms that allow computers to learn from and make predictions based on data. The primary goal of machine learning is to enable systems to improve their performance on tasks over time without being explicitly programmed. This ability to learn from data and adapt to new situations is what makes machine learning so powerful and versatile.

Machine learning can be broadly categorized into three main types: supervised learning, unsupervised learning, and reinforcement learning. Each type has its own set of techniques, and challenges.

Supervised Learning

Supervised learning is the most commonly used type of machine learning. In supervised learning, the algorithm is trained on a labeled dataset, which means that each training example is paired with an output label. The goal of the algorithm is to learn a mapping from inputs to outputs so that it can predict the output for new, unseen inputs.

Techniques in Supervised Learning

Linear Regression: Linear regression is used for predicting continuous outcomes. It models the relationship between a dependent variable and one or more independent variables by fitting a linear equation to observed data. Despite its simplicity, linear regression can be very effective for many applications, such as predicting house prices or stock prices.

Logistic Regression: Logistic regression is used for binary classification problems. It models the probability that a given input belongs to a particular class. Logistic regression is widely used in fields like medicine, for predicting whether a patient has a certain disease, and in marketing, for predicting whether a customer will purchase a product.

Decision Trees: Decision trees are used for both classification and regression tasks. They work by recursively splitting the data into subsets based on the value of an attribute, forming a tree-like structure. Decision trees are easy to interpret and can handle both numerical and categorical data. However, they can be prone to overfitting, especially when the tree is very deep.

Support Vector Machines (SVMs): SVMs are powerful classification algorithms that find the hyperplane that best separates different classes in the feature space. They are particularly effective in high-dimensional spaces and are used for tasks such as image classification and text categorization.

Neural Networks: Neural networks are a type of supervised learning algorithm that are particularly powerful for complex tasks such as image and speech recognition. They consist of layers of interconnected nodes, or neurons, that process data in a way that mimics the human brain.

Challenges in Supervised Learning

Supervised learning requires a large amount of labeled data, which can be expensive and time-consuming to obtain. Additionally, the algorithm's performance can be highly dependent on the quality of the data. Noise in the data, such as mislabeled examples or irrelevant features, can significantly degrade the algorithm's performance. Overfitting is another common challenge, where the model learns the training data too well and performs poorly on new, unseen data.

Unsupervised Learning

Unsupervised learning involves training algorithms on unlabeled data, where the goal is to identify patterns or structures within the data. Unlike supervised learning, there are no output labels to guide the learning process.

Techniques in Unsupervised Learning

Clustering: Clustering algorithms group similar data points together. The most well-known clustering algorithm is k-means, which partitions the data into k clusters by minimizing the variance within each cluster. Clustering is used in applications such as customer segmentation, image compression, and anomaly detection.

Dimensionality Reduction: Dimensionality reduction techniques, such as Principal Component Analysis (PCA) and t-Distributed Stochastic Neighbor Embedding (t-SNE), reduce the number of features in the data while preserving its essential structure. These techniques are used to visualize high-dimensional data and to reduce the computational complexity of machine learning algorithms.

Association Rules: Association rule learning is used to identify relationships between variables in large datasets. The most famous algorithm for association rule learning is the Apriori algorithm, which is used in market basket analysis to find sets of products that frequently co-occur in transactions.

Autoencoders: Autoencoders are a type of neural network used for unsupervised learning. They work by compressing the input data into a lower-dimensional representation and then reconstructing the original data from this representation. Autoencoders are used for tasks such as anomaly detection and data denoising.

Challenges in Unsupervised Learning

Unsupervised learning can be more challenging than supervised learning because there is no straightforward way to evaluate the performance of the algorithm. Additionally, the patterns identified by unsupervised learning algorithms may not always be meaningful or useful for the task at hand. Selecting the appropriate algorithm and tuning its parameters can also be more difficult without labeled data to guide the process.

Reinforcement Learning

Reinforcement learning is a type of machine learning where an agent learns to make decisions by interacting with an environment. The agent receives feedback in the form of rewards or penalties based on its actions and aims to maximize the cumulative reward over time.

Techniques in Reinforcement Learning

Q-Learning: Q-learning is a model-free reinforcement learning algorithm that learns the value of each action in a given state. The agent updates its knowledge based on the rewards received and uses this knowledge to choose actions that maximize future rewards. Q-learning is used in applications such as game playing and robotic control.

Deep Q-Networks (DQNs): DQNs combine Q-learning with deep learning, using neural networks to approximate the Q-values. This approach allows the agent to handle high-dimensional state spaces, such as those encountered in video games.

Policy Gradient Methods: Policy gradient methods directly learn a policy that maps states to actions, rather than learning the value of each action. These methods can handle continuous action spaces and are used in applications such as robotic manipulation and autonomous driving.

Actor-Critic Methods: Actor-critic methods combine the advantages of value-based and policy-based methods. The actor learns the policy, while the critic estimates the value function. This approach can improve learning stability and convergence.

Challenges in Reinforcement Learning

Reinforcement learning can be computationally expensive and time-consuming, as the agent needs to explore the environment and gather experience. The exploration-exploitation trade-off is a fundamental challenge, where the agent must balance exploring new actions to discover their rewards with exploiting known actions to maximize rewards. Additionally, designing the reward function is critical, as it can significantly impact the agent's behavior and learning efficiency.

Neural Networks

Neural networks are the cornerstone of many modern artificial intelligence applications. Inspired by the structure and function of the human brain, neural networks consist of interconnected nodes, or neurons, that work together to process and learn from data. This section explores the fundamental components of neural networks, their various types, and the techniques used to train and optimize them.

Structure of Neural Networks

A neural network is composed of layers of neurons. These layers include an input layer, one or more hidden layers, and an output layer. Each neuron in a layer is connected to neurons in the subsequent layer through weighted connections. The weights are adjustable parameters that the network learns during the training process.

Neurons and Activation Functions

Neurons are the basic units of a neural network. Each neuron receives input from multiple neurons in the previous layer, applies a weighted sum to these inputs, adds a bias term, and then passes the result through an activation function. The activation function introduces non-linearity into the network, enabling it to learn complex patterns.

Common activation functions include:

Sigmoid: The sigmoid function maps input values to the range (0, 1), making it useful for binary classification tasks. However, it can suffer from the vanishing gradient problem during training.

Tanh: The tanh function maps input values to the range (-1, 1). It often performs better than the sigmoid function but can still suffer from the vanishing gradient problem.

ReLU (Rectified Linear Unit): The ReLU function maps positive input values to themselves and negative input values to zero. ReLU is widely used due to its ability to mitigate the vanishing gradient problem and improve training efficiency.

Leaky ReLU: Leaky ReLU is a variant of ReLU that allows a small, non-zero gradient for negative input values. This helps prevent dead neurons during training.

Softmax: The softmax function is used in the output layer for multi-class classification tasks. It converts the raw output scores into probabilities that sum to one.

Layers of a Neural Network

Input Layer: The input layer receives the raw data and passes it to the subsequent hidden layers. The number of neurons in the input layer corresponds to the number of features in the data.

Hidden Layers: Hidden layers perform intermediate computations and extract features from the input data. The number of hidden layers and neurons per layer can vary depending on the complexity of the task and the architecture of the network.

Output Layer: The output layer produces the final prediction or classification. The number of neurons in the output layer depends on the specific task, such as the number of classes in a classification problem.

Types of Neural Networks

Neural networks come in various architectures, each suited for different types of tasks and data. Here, we explore some of the most common types of neural networks.

Feedforward Neural Networks (FNNs)

Feedforward neural networks are the simplest type of neural network, where data flows in one direction from the input layer to the output layer through hidden layers. FNNs are used for tasks such as image and speech recognition. They are also known as multi-layer perceptrons (MLPs) when they consist of multiple hidden layers.

Convolutional Neural Networks (CNNs)

Convolutional neural networks are designed for processing grid-like data, such as images. CNNs use convolutional layers to automatically detect features like edges, textures, and shapes. Key components of CNNs include:

Convolutional Layers: Convolutional layers apply a set of filters to the input data, producing feature maps that highlight important patterns. The filters are learned during the training process.

Pooling Layers: Pooling layers downsample the feature maps, reducing their spatial dimensions and computational complexity. Common pooling operations include max pooling and average pooling.

Fully Connected Layers: After several convolutional and pooling layers, the feature maps are flattened and passed through fully connected layers for classification or regression tasks.

Dropout Layers: Dropout layers randomly set a fraction of the neurons to zero during training, helping to prevent overfitting by introducing regularization.

Recurrent Neural Networks (RNNs)

Recurrent neural networks are designed for sequential data, such as time series or natural language. RNNs maintain a hidden state that captures information about previous inputs, allowing them to model dependencies over time. Key components of RNNs include:

Hidden State: The hidden state is a memory that stores information from previous time steps. It is updated at each time step based on the current input and the previous hidden state.

Long Short-Term Memory (LSTM): LSTM networks are a type of RNN designed to address the vanishing gradient problem. They use gates to control the flow of information, allowing them to capture long-term dependencies.

Gated Recurrent Unit (GRU): GRUs are a simplified version of LSTMs that use fewer gates but still effectively capture long-term dependencies.

Transformer Models

Transformer models have revolutionized natural language processing by introducing a novel architecture that relies on self-attention mechanisms. Key components of transformer models include:

Self-Attention Mechanism: Self-attention allows the model to weigh the importance of different input tokens when making predictions. It enables the model to capture dependencies between distant tokens more effectively than RNNs.

Encoder-Decoder Architecture: Transformer models often use an encoder-decoder architecture for tasks such as translation. The encoder processes the input sequence, and the decoder generates the output sequence based on the encoder's representation.

Positional Encoding: Since transformers do not have a built-in notion of sequence order, positional encodings are added to the input embeddings to provide information about the relative positions of tokens.

Training Neural Networks

Training a neural network involves adjusting its weights based on the data to minimize a loss function. This process requires significant computational resources and can be optimized using various techniques.

Forward Propagation

Forward propagation is the process by which input data is passed through the network to generate predictions. During forward propagation, each neuron's output is calculated by applying the activation function to the weighted sum of its inputs. The outputs are passed through the layers until the final prediction is produced.

Loss Function

The loss function measures the difference between the network's predictions and the actual labels. The choice of loss function depends on the specific task:

Mean Squared Error (MSE): Used for regression tasks, MSE measures the average squared difference between the predicted and actual values.

Cross-Entropy Loss: Used for classification tasks, cross-entropy loss measures the difference between the predicted probability distribution and the true distribution.

Hinge Loss: Used for binary classification tasks, hinge loss is commonly associated with support vector machines. It penalizes predictions that are on the wrong side of the decision boundary.

Backpropagation

Backpropagation is an algorithm used to calculate the gradients of the loss function with respect to the network's weights. It propagates the error backward through the network, enabling efficient computation of gradients and updating weights accordingly.

The backpropagation process involves two main steps:

Backward Pass: The gradient of the loss function is computed with respect to each weight by applying the chain rule of calculus. This process involves calculating the partial derivatives of the loss with respect to the weights, starting from the output layer and moving backward through the hidden layers.

Weight Update: The weights are updated using an optimization algorithm, such as gradient descent. The weights are adjusted in the direction that reduces the loss, based on the computed gradients.

Optimization Algorithms

Optimization algorithms are used to update the weights of the neural network during training. Common optimization algorithms include:

Gradient Descent: Gradient descent iteratively updates the weights to minimize the loss function. Variants of gradient descent, such as stochastic gradient descent (SGD) and mini-batch gradient descent, improve convergence speed and stability.

Momentum: Momentum is an extension of gradient descent that accumulates an exponentially decaying moving average of past gradients. This helps accelerate convergence and smooth out oscillations.

Adaptive Learning Rate Methods: Adaptive learning rate methods, such as AdaGrad, RMSprop, and Adam, adjust the learning rate for each parameter based on past gradients. These methods can improve convergence speed and stability.

Regularization Techniques

Regularization techniques are used to prevent overfitting and improve the generalization ability of neural networks. Common regularization techniques include:

L1 and L2 Regularization: L1 regularization adds the absolute values of the weights to the loss function, encouraging sparsity. L2 regularization adds the squared values of the weights, encouraging smaller weights and reducing overfitting.

Dropout: Dropout randomly sets a fraction of the neurons to zero during training, preventing the network from relying too heavily on any single neuron and improving generalization.

Batch Normalization: Batch normalization normalizes the inputs to each layer, reducing internal covariate shift and improving training stability and convergence.

Hyperparameter Tuning

Hyperparameters are parameters that are not learned during training but are set before the training process begins. Examples include the learning rate, batch size, and the number of layers and neurons. Hyperparameter tuning involves searching for the optimal set of hyperparameters to achieve the best performance on a given task.

Common techniques for hyperparameter tuning include:

Grid Search: Grid search involves exhaustively searching through a predefined set of hyperparameters. While comprehensive, it can be computationally expensive.

Random Search: Random search involves randomly sampling hyperparameters from a predefined distribution. It is often more efficient than grid search and can explore a larger hyperparameter space.

Bayesian Optimization: Bayesian optimization uses probabilistic models to guide the search for optimal hyperparameters. It balances exploration and exploitation to find the best hyperparameters efficiently.

Natural Language Processing (NLP)

Natural Language Processing (NLP) is a field of AI focused on enabling machines to understand, interpret, and generate human language. NLP techniques are essential for creating AI agents that can interact with humans through text or speech.

Text Analysis Techniques

Text analysis involves preprocessing and transforming raw text data into a format suitable for machine learning algorithms. Key techniques include:

Tokenization

Tokenization is the process of breaking down text into individual words or phrases, known as tokens. This step is crucial for analyzing and processing text data in NLP applications.

Stemming and Lemmatization

Stemming reduces words to their base or root form, while lemmatization maps words to their dictionary form. These techniques help normalize text data, reducing variations and improving the accuracy of NLP models.

Part-of-Speech Tagging

Part-of-speech tagging assigns grammatical labels (e.g., noun, verb, adjective) to each word in a text. This information is useful for understanding the syntactic structure and meaning of sentences.

Sentiment Analysis

Sentiment analysis involves determining the sentiment or emotion expressed in a piece of text. This technique is widely used in social media monitoring, customer feedback analysis, and market research.

Rule-Based Approaches

Rule-based approaches use predefined rules and lexicons to identify sentiment in text. While simple and interpretable, these methods often struggle with nuances and context.

Machine Learning Approaches

Machine learning approaches train models on labeled data to predict sentiment. These methods, including logistic regression, support vector machines, and neural networks, can capture complex patterns and improve accuracy.

Deep Learning Approaches

Deep learning models, such as CNNs and RNNs, have shown significant improvements in sentiment analysis. These models can automatically learn features from raw text data, capturing subtle nuances and context.

Language Generation

Language generation involves creating human-like text based on a given input. Applications include chatbots, content creation, and translation.

Rule-Based Approaches

Rule-based approaches use predefined templates and rules to generate text. While simple and controllable, these methods often produce rigid and repetitive outputs.

Statistical Approaches

Statistical approaches, such as n-gram models and Markov chains, generate text based on the probabilities of word sequences. These methods can capture more natural language patterns but may still lack coherence.

Neural Network Approaches

Neural network models, such as RNNs and transformers, have revolutionized language generation. These models can generate coherent, contextually relevant text by learning from large datasets. Transformer-based models like GPT-4 have set new benchmarks in language generation tasks.

Speech Recognition and Synthesis

Speech recognition and synthesis are crucial components of NLP, enabling voice-activated assistants, transcription services, and accessible communication tools.

Automatic Speech Recognition (ASR)

ASR systems convert spoken language into text. Modern ASR systems use deep learning models, such as CNNs and RNNs, to achieve high accuracy in various languages and accents.

Text-to-Speech (TTS)

TTS systems convert text into spoken language. Advances in deep learning have enabled TTS systems to generate natural-sounding speech with accurate intonation and emotion. Techniques like WaveNet and Tacotron have set new standards in TTS quality

Automation Systems

Automation and robotics are integral to AI agents, enabling them to perform tasks traditionally done by humans. These systems leverage various AI technologies to control processes, manage workflows, and optimize operations.

Robotic Process Automation (RPA)

RPA involves using AI agents to automate repetitive tasks in business processes, such as data entry, invoice processing, and customer support. RPA improves productivity and accuracy while freeing up human workers for more strategic tasks.

Components of RPA

Bot Creation: RPA bots are created using specialized software tools that allow users to define workflows and automate tasks without extensive programming knowledge.

Workflow Automation: RPA bots follow predefined workflows to perform tasks, such as data extraction, form filling, and report generation. These workflows can be customized to meet specific business needs.

Integration with Systems: RPA bots can integrate with various enterprise systems, such as CRM, ERP, and databases, to streamline processes and improve efficiency.

Industrial Automation

Industrial automation involves using AI agents to control manufacturing processes, optimize production lines, and ensure quality control. This automation improves efficiency, reduces costs, and enhances product quality.

Key Technologies in Industrial Automation

Programmable Logic Controllers (PLCs): PLCs are specialized computers used to control industrial processes. They can be programmed to perform specific tasks, such as monitoring sensors, controlling machinery, and managing production lines.

Supervisory Control and Data Acquisition (SCADA): SCADA systems provide real-time monitoring and control of industrial processes. They collect data from sensors and equipment, allowing operators to make informed decisions and optimize operations.

Industrial Robots: Industrial robots are used for tasks such as assembly, welding, painting, and packaging. These robots can work with high precision and speed, improving productivity and product quality.

Service Automation

Service automation involves using AI-powered robots to assist in healthcare, hospitality, and retail environments. These robots can perform tasks such as patient care, cleaning, and inventory management, improving service quality and efficiency.

Applications of Service Robots

Healthcare: Service robots assist healthcare professionals by performing tasks such as patient monitoring, medication dispensing, and surgical assistance. These robots can improve patient outcomes and reduce the workload on healthcare staff.

Hospitality: In the hospitality industry, service robots are used for tasks such as room service, cleaning, and guest assistance. These robots enhance the guest experience by providing efficient and personalized services.

Retail: Service robots in retail environments help with inventory management, customer assistance, and checkout processes. These robots can improve operational efficiency and enhance the shopping experience for customers.

Autonomous Systems

Autonomous systems, such as self-driving cars and drones, leverage AI agents to navigate and operate independently. These technologies have applications in transportation, logistics, agriculture, and defense.

Key Components of Autonomous Systems

Perception: Autonomous systems use sensors, such as cameras, LiDAR, and radar, to perceive their environment. AI algorithms process this sensor data to detect objects, recognize patterns, and understand the environment.

Localization and Mapping: Autonomous systems use techniques like Simultaneous Localization and Mapping (SLAM) to create maps of their environment and determine their position within these maps. This information is crucial for navigation and path planning.

Decision Making: AI agents in autonomous systems make decisions based on sensor data and environmental maps. These decisions include route planning, obstacle avoidance, and task execution.

Control and Actuation: Autonomous systems use control algorithms to execute decisions and control actuators, such as motors and steering mechanisms. These algorithms ensure smooth and safe operation.

Ethical and Safety Considerations

As automation and robotics become more prevalent, ethical and safety considerations are paramount. Ensuring that AI agents operate safely and ethically is crucial for gaining public trust and acceptance.

Ethical Considerations

Job Displacement: Automation can lead to job displacement, particularly in industries with high levels of repetitive tasks. Addressing the social and economic impacts of job displacement is essential for ethical AI deployment.

Bias and Fairness: Ensuring that AI agents operate fairly and without bias is crucial. This includes addressing biases in training data and developing algorithms that promote fairness and equality.

Transparency and Accountability: AI agents should operate transparently and be accountable for their actions. This includes providing explanations for decisions and ensuring that there are mechanisms for addressing errors and grievances.

Safety Considerations

Robustness and Reliability: AI agents must be robust and reliable, particularly in critical applications like healthcare and autonomous systems. This includes rigorous testing and validation to ensure safe operation.

Human Oversight: Maintaining human oversight of AI agents is crucial for safety. This includes ensuring that humans can intervene and take control if necessary.

Regulation and Standards: Developing and adhering to regulations and standards for AI and robotics is essential for ensuring safety and ethical operation. This includes collaborating with regulatory bodies and industry organizations.

Dive Deep: Machine Learning and Neural Networks

Machine learning (ML) and neural networks are the backbone of AI agents, providing the computational power and intelligence necessary to learn from data, make predictions, and improve over time. This section delves deeply into the principles, techniques, and architectures of machine learning and neural networks, providing a comprehensive understanding of how they work and their applications.

Machine Learning Fundamentals

Machine learning is a subset of artificial intelligence that focuses on developing algorithms that allow computers to learn from and make predictions based on data. The primary goal of machine learning is to enable systems to improve their performance on tasks over time without being explicitly programmed.

Types of Machine Learning

Machine learning can be broadly categorized into three main types: supervised learning, unsupervised learning, and reinforcement learning.

Supervised Learning

Supervised learning is a core area of machine learning where models are trained on labeled data. This approach involves using input-output pairs, where the input data is provided along with the correct output. The goal is for the model to learn a mapping from inputs to outputs and make accurate predictions on new, unseen data. Supervised learning is foundational for many real-world applications, including image recognition, speech recognition, and medical diagnosis.

Key Concepts in Supervised Learning

1. **Training Data**: The dataset used to train the model, consisting of input features and corresponding labels.
2. **Validation Data**: A subset of the data used to tune model parameters and select the best model.
3. **Test Data**: A separate dataset used to evaluate the model's performance after training.
4. **Model**: A mathematical representation of the relationship between inputs and outputs.
5. **Objective Function**: A function used to evaluate the performance of the model, often referred to as the loss or cost function.

Types of Supervised Learning Algorithms

Supervised learning algorithms can be broadly categorized into regression and classification algorithms.

Regression Algorithms

Regression algorithms predict a continuous output variable based on input features. They are used in scenarios where the goal is to predict a numerical value.

1. **Linear Regression**: This algorithm models the relationship between a dependent variable and one or more independent variables by fitting a line to observed data. It is widely used for predicting outcomes such as house prices, stock prices, and sales forecasting.
2. **Polynomial Regression**: An extension of linear regression that models the relationship between the variables as an nth degree polynomial. It captures more complex, non-linear relationships.
3. **Ridge and Lasso Regression**: These variants of linear regression include regularization terms to prevent

overfitting. Ridge regression adds a penalty for the size of the coefficients, while Lasso regression encourages simpler models by penalizing the absolute size of the coefficients.

4. **Decision Trees for Regression**: Decision trees split the data into subsets based on the value of an attribute, forming a tree-like structure. Each split aims to minimize variance within the subsets.

5. **Support Vector Regression (SVR)**: SVR uses a margin of tolerance within which errors are not penalized, aiming to find the best fit line that lies within this margin.

6. **Neural Networks for Regression**: Neural networks consist of layers of interconnected nodes (neurons) that process data in a way that mimics the human brain. They are particularly powerful for capturing complex patterns in large datasets.

Classification Algorithms

Classification algorithms predict a discrete output variable (class label) based on input features. They are used in scenarios where the goal is to categorize input data into one or more predefined classes.

1. **Logistic Regression**: Despite its name, logistic regression is used for binary classification tasks. It models the probability that a given input belongs to a particular class, making it useful for applications like spam detection and disease diagnosis.

2. **Decision Trees for Classification**: Decision trees for classification split the data into subsets based on the value of an attribute and assign a class label to each subset. The splits are chosen to maximize information gain or minimize impurity.

3. **Random Forests**: An ensemble method that builds multiple decision trees and combines their predictions. Random forests improve the accuracy and robustness of decision trees by reducing overfitting.

4. **Support Vector Machines (SVMs)**: SVMs find the hyperplane that best separates different classes in the feature space. For non-linearly separable data, SVMs use kernel functions to project the data into a higher-dimensional space.

5. **K-Nearest Neighbors (KNN)**: A simple, instance-based learning algorithm that classifies a new input based on the majority class of its k-nearest neighbors in the training data.

6. **Naive Bayes**: A probabilistic classifier based on Bayes' theorem, assuming independence between features. It is particularly effective for text classification tasks.

7. **Neural Networks for Classification**: Neural networks for classification use layers of neurons to process inputs and outputs. The final layer typically uses a softmax function to produce probabilities for each class.

Model Evaluation and Validation

Evaluating and validating supervised learning models is crucial to ensure their generalizability to new data. Common evaluation metrics include:

1. **Accuracy**: The ratio of correctly predicted instances to the total number of instances, used for classification tasks.

2. **Precision, Recall, and F1 Score**: Precision is the ratio of true positives to the sum of true positives and false positives. Recall is the ratio of true positives to the sum of true positives and false negatives. The F1 score is the harmonic mean of precision and recall.

3. **Mean Squared Error (MSE)**: Used for regression tasks, MSE measures the average squared difference between predicted and actual values.

4. **Confusion Matrix**: A table used to evaluate the performance of a classification model, showing the true

positives, true negatives, false positives, and false negatives.

5. **ROC Curve and AUC**: The Receiver Operating Characteristic (ROC) curve plots the true positive rate against the false positive rate at various threshold settings. The Area Under the Curve (AUC) measures the overall performance of the classification model.

Cross-Validation

Cross-validation is a technique used to assess the generalizability of a model. The data is split into k subsets, and the model is trained on k-1 subsets and tested on the remaining subset. This process is repeated k times, with each subset serving as the test set once. The performance metrics are averaged over the k iterations to obtain a more robust estimate.

k-Fold Cross-Validation: The most common form of cross-validation, where the data is divided into k equal-sized subsets.

Leave-One-Out Cross-Validation (LOOCV): A special case of k-fold cross-validation where k equals the number of instances in the dataset. Each instance serves as the test set exactly once.

Stratified k-Fold Cross-Validation: Ensures that each fold has a representative proportion of each class, used for imbalanced datasets.

Hyperparameter Tuning

Hyperparameter tuning involves searching for the optimal set of hyperparameters for a model. This process is essential for improving model performance and involves techniques such as:

Grid Search: An exhaustive search over a specified parameter grid. While comprehensive, it can be computationally expensive.

Random Search: Samples hyperparameters from a specified distribution. It is often more efficient than grid search and can explore a larger hyperparameter space.

Bayesian Optimization: Uses probabilistic models to guide the search for optimal hyperparameters, balancing exploration and exploitation to find the best set efficiently.

Advanced Topics in Supervised Learning
Ensemble Methods

Ensemble methods combine the predictions of multiple models to improve accuracy and robustness.

Bagging: Bootstrap Aggregating (Bagging) involves training multiple models on different bootstrap samples of the data and averaging their predictions. Random Forests are a popular example of bagging.

Boosting: Boosting involves sequentially training models, with each new model focusing on the errors made by the previous models. AdaBoost and Gradient Boosting Machines (GBM) are common boosting algorithms.

Stacking: Stacking involves training multiple models (base learners) and using their predictions as input to a meta-learner, which makes the final prediction.

Model Interpretability

Understanding and interpreting machine learning models is crucial for gaining insights and ensuring trust in the predictions.

Feature Importance: Measures the contribution of each feature to the model's predictions. Techniques such as permutation importance and SHAP (SHapley Additive exPlanations) are used to estimate feature importance.

Partial Dependence Plots: Show the relationship between a feature and the predicted outcome, holding other features constant.

LIME (Local Interpretable Model-agnostic Explanations): Explains individual predictions by approximating the model locally with an interpretable model.

Rule Extraction: Converts the learned model into a set of human-readable rules, often used for decision trees and rule-based models.

Applications of Supervised Learning

Supervised learning has a wide range of applications across various domains, demonstrating its versatility and potential to transform different fields.

1) **Healthcare**: Predicting patient outcomes, diagnosing diseases, and personalizing treatment plans.
2) **Finance**: Credit scoring, fraud detection, and algorithmic trading.
3) **Marketing**: Customer segmentation, sentiment analysis, and personalized recommendations.
4) **Retail**: Demand forecasting, inventory management, and sales prediction.
5) **Manufacturing**: Predictive maintenance, quality control, and process optimization.
6) **Security**: Intrusion detection, spam filtering, and biometric authentication.

Unsupervised Learning

Unsupervised learning is a type of machine learning where the algorithm is trained on data without labeled responses. The goal is to uncover hidden patterns, structures, and relationships within the data. Unlike supervised learning, unsupervised learning does not rely on input-output pairs and is often used for exploratory data analysis, clustering, and dimensionality reduction.

Key Concepts in Unsupervised Learning

1. **Data Without Labels**: In unsupervised learning, the dataset consists solely of input data without corresponding output labels. The algorithm seeks to identify patterns and relationships within the data.
2. **Learning from Data**: The algorithm learns the underlying structure of the data through various techniques, allowing for the discovery of natural groupings and features.
3. **Applications**: Common applications of unsupervised learning include customer segmentation, anomaly detection, and data compression.

Types of Unsupervised Learning Algorithms

Unsupervised learning algorithms can be broadly categorized into clustering, dimensionality reduction, and association rule learning.

Clustering Algorithms

Clustering algorithms group similar data points into clusters based on certain criteria, such as distance or density. These algorithms are used in applications like market segmentation, image compression, and bioinformatics.

1. **K-Means Clustering**

Algorithm: K-means clustering partitions the data into K clusters, where each data point belongs to the cluster with the nearest mean. The algorithm iteratively updates cluster centroids and reassigns data points until convergence.

Advantages: Simple and easy to implement, efficient for large datasets.

Challenges: Requires the number of clusters (K) to be specified in advance, sensitive to initial centroid placement, may converge to local minima.

2. Hierarchical Clustering

Algorithm: Hierarchical clustering builds a tree-like structure (dendrogram) by iteratively merging or splitting clusters. There are two main approaches: agglomerative (bottom-up) and divisive (top-down).

Advantages: Does not require the number of clusters to be specified, produces a hierarchy of clusters.

Challenges: Computationally intensive for large datasets, choosing the level at which to cut the dendrogram can be subjective.

3. DBSCAN (Density-Based Spatial Clustering of Applications with Noise)

Algorithm: DBSCAN clusters data points based on density, identifying regions of high density separated by regions of low density. It can detect clusters of arbitrary shapes and handle noise.

Advantages: Does not require specifying the number of clusters, robust to noise and outliers, can find clusters of arbitrary shape.

Challenges: Sensitive to the choice of hyperparameters (epsilon and minimum points), performance can degrade with varying density in data.

4. Gaussian Mixture Models (GMM)

Algorithm: GMM assumes that the data is generated from a mixture of several Gaussian distributions. It uses the Expectation-Maximization (EM) algorithm to estimate the parameters of these distributions.

Advantages: Can model clusters of different shapes and sizes, provides probabilistic cluster assignments.

Challenges: Requires specifying the number of components, can be sensitive to initialization, computationally intensive.

Dimensionality Reduction Algorithms

Dimensionality reduction algorithms transform high-dimensional data into a lower-dimensional space while preserving important structures and relationships. These algorithms are used for data visualization, noise reduction, and feature extraction.

1.   **Principal Component Analysis (PCA)**

Algorithm: PCA identifies the principal components (directions of maximum variance) in the data and projects the data onto these components. It reduces the dimensionality by keeping only the most significant components.

Advantages: Simple and computationally efficient, widely used for data visualization and noise reduction.

Challenges: Assumes linear relationships between variables, may not capture complex structures.

2.   **t-Distributed Stochastic Neighbor Embedding (t-SNE)**

Algorithm: t-SNE is a non-linear dimensionality reduction technique that preserves the local structure of the data. It maps high-dimensional data to a lower-dimensional space (typically 2D or 3D) for visualization.

Advantages: Effective for visualizing complex datasets, captures non-linear relationships.

Challenges: Computationally expensive, sensitive to hyperparameters, primarily used for visualization rather than feature extraction.

3. **Autoencoders**

Algorithm: Autoencoders are neural networks designed to learn efficient representations of data. They consist of an encoder that compresses the data into a lower-dimensional representation and a decoder that reconstructs the original data from this representation.

Advantages: Can capture complex non-linear relationships, useful for unsupervised feature learning and data denoising.

Challenges: Requires careful tuning of network architecture and hyperparameters, training can be computationally intensive.

Association Rule Learning

Association rule learning algorithms discover interesting relationships between variables in large datasets. These algorithms are commonly used in market basket analysis to identify frequently co-occurring items.

1. **Apriori Algorithm**

Algorithm: The Apriori algorithm identifies frequent itemsets (sets of items that frequently occur together) and generates association rules based on these itemsets. It uses a bottom-up approach, gradually expanding itemsets and pruning infrequent ones.

Advantages: Simple and easy to implement, useful for discovering common patterns in transactional data.

Challenges: Can be computationally expensive for large datasets, may generate a large number of rules, some of which may be trivial.

2.   **FP-Growth (Frequent Pattern Growth)**

Algorithm: FP-Growth is an efficient alternative to the Apriori algorithm. It constructs a compact data structure called an FP-tree and extracts frequent itemsets directly from this tree without candidate generation.

Advantages: Faster than Apriori for large datasets, reduces the number of database scans.

Challenges: Implementation can be complex, still generates many rules that need to be filtered for relevance.

Model Evaluation and Validation

Evaluating unsupervised learning models is more challenging than supervised learning because there are no ground truth labels to compare against. Common evaluation methods include:

1.   **Silhouette Score**: Measures how similar an object is to its own cluster compared to other clusters. A higher silhouette score indicates better-defined clusters.
2.   **Davies-Bouldin Index**: Evaluates the average similarity ratio of each cluster with its most similar cluster. Lower values indicate better clustering.
3.   **Elbow Method**: Used to determine the optimal number of clusters in K-means by plotting the explained variance as a function of the number of clusters and looking for an "elbow" point where the rate of variance explained starts to diminish.

4.   **Cluster Validity Indices**: Metrics like the Dunn index, Rand index, and Adjusted Rand Index assess the quality of clustering by comparing intra-cluster compactness and inter-cluster separation.

Advanced Topics in Unsupervised Learning

Semi-Supervised Learning

Semi-supervised learning combines supervised and unsupervised learning techniques to leverage both labeled and unlabeled data. It is useful when labeled data is scarce or expensive to obtain.

1.   **Self-Training**: A semi-supervised learning approach where the model is initially trained on labeled data and then used to label the unlabeled data. The newly labeled data is then used to retrain the model.
2.   **Co-Training**: Involves training two separate models on different views of the data and allowing them to label unlabeled data for each other.
3.   **Generative Models**: Use models like Variational Autoencoders (VAEs) or Generative Adversarial Networks (GANs) to generate new data points and improve the learning process.

Anomaly Detection

Anomaly detection identifies rare or unusual patterns in data that do not conform to expected behavior. It is widely used in fraud detection, network security, and fault detection.

1.   **Statistical Methods**: Techniques like Z-score, Grubbs' test, and Gaussian distribution identify anomalies based on statistical properties of the data.
2.   **Machine Learning Methods**: Algorithms like Isolation Forest, One-Class SVM, and Autoencoders detect anomalies by learning the normal patterns in the data and flagging deviations.
3.   **Ensemble Methods**: Combine multiple anomaly detection techniques to improve robustness and accuracy.

Applications of Unsupervised Learning

Unsupervised learning is applied across various domains to uncover hidden patterns and structures in data.

1. **Customer Segmentation**: Grouping customers based on purchasing behavior, demographics, or other attributes to tailor marketing strategies.
2. **Image Compression**: Reducing the dimensionality of image data for efficient storage and transmission.
3. **Genomics**: Identifying gene expressions and similarities between different biological samples.
4. **Recommendation Systems**: Discovering latent factors in user-item interactions to improve recommendations.
5. **Market Basket Analysis**: Finding associations between products in transaction data to optimize product placement and cross-selling strategies.
6. **Social Network Analysis**: Detecting communities and influential nodes within social networks.

Reinforcement Learning

Reinforcement learning (RL) is a type of machine learning where an agent learns to make decisions by interacting with an environment. The agent receives feedback in the form of rewards or penalties and aims to maximize the cumulative reward over time. Unlike supervised learning, which relies on labeled data, reinforcement learning is based on trial and error, allowing the agent to learn from its own experiences.

Key Concepts in Reinforcement Learning

1. **Agent**: The entity that learns and makes decisions by interacting with the environment.

2. **Environment**: The external system with which the agent interacts. The environment provides feedback to the agent based on its actions.
3. **State**: A representation of the current situation or configuration of the environment.
4. **Action**: A decision or move made by the agent that affects the state of the environment.
5. **Reward**: A scalar feedback signal given to the agent to evaluate its action. Positive rewards encourage certain behaviors, while negative rewards discourage others.
6. **Policy**: A strategy or mapping from states to actions, guiding the agent's behavior.
7. **Value Function**: A function that estimates the expected cumulative reward of being in a particular state or taking a specific action.
8. **Q-Function**: Also known as the action-value function, it estimates the expected cumulative reward of taking a particular action in a given state.

Types of Reinforcement Learning

Reinforcement learning can be categorized into model-based and model-free methods.

Model-Based RL: The agent builds a model of the environment to predict the outcomes of its actions. This model is used to plan and make decisions.

Model-Free RL: The agent learns a policy or value function directly from its interactions with the environment, without building an explicit model.

Model-Free RL Algorithms

Q-Learning: A popular model-free algorithm that learns the action-value function (Q-function) to estimate the expected cumulative reward of taking an action in a given state. The Q-function is updated iteratively using the Bellman equation.

Deep Q-Networks (DQNs): An extension of Q-learning that uses deep neural networks to approximate the Q-function. DQNs have been successfully applied to complex tasks, such as playing video games.

Policy Gradient Methods: These methods directly optimize the policy by adjusting the parameters of a neural network. Common algorithms include REINFORCE, Actor-Critic, and Proximal Policy Optimization (PPO).

SARSA (State-Action-Reward-State-Action): An on-policy algorithm that updates the Q-function based on the action taken by the current policy. Unlike Q-learning, which is off-policy, SARSA learns the value of the policy being followed.

Components of Reinforcement Learning

Exploration vs. Exploitation: Balancing the exploration of new actions to discover their rewards with the exploitation of known actions to maximize the cumulative reward. Techniques like epsilon-greedy and softmax are used to manage this trade-off.

Temporal Difference Learning: A method that updates value estimates based on the difference between consecutive predictions. It combines ideas from Monte Carlo methods and dynamic programming.

Discount Factor (γ): A parameter that determines the importance of future rewards. A discount factor close to 1 values future rewards similarly to immediate rewards, while a discount factor close to 0 prioritizes immediate rewards.

Reward Shaping: Modifying the reward function to provide more informative feedback to the agent, facilitating faster learning.

Deep Reinforcement Learning

Deep reinforcement learning combines reinforcement learning with deep learning techniques, enabling the agent to learn from high-dimensional sensory inputs, such as images and videos. This combination has led to significant advancements in various fields, including robotics, gaming, and autonomous systems.

Applications of Deep RL

Gaming: Deep RL has achieved superhuman performance in games like Go, Chess, and various Atari games. Notable examples include AlphaGo, AlphaZero, and DQN.

Robotics: Deep RL is used to train robots for tasks such as manipulation, navigation, and locomotion. It allows robots to learn from raw sensory data and adapt to complex environments.

Autonomous Vehicles: Deep RL enables self-driving cars to learn driving policies by interacting with simulated environments. It helps in decision-making, path planning, and obstacle avoidance.

Healthcare: Deep RL is used for personalized treatment planning, optimizing clinical trials, and managing healthcare resources.

Advanced Topics in Reinforcement Learning

Multi-Agent Reinforcement Learning (MARL): Involves multiple agents interacting in a shared environment, learning to collaborate or compete to achieve their goals. Applications include autonomous driving fleets and coordinated robotics.

Inverse Reinforcement Learning (IRL): The goal is to infer the reward function from observed behavior. It is useful for understanding human preferences and replicating expert behavior.

Transfer Learning: Leveraging knowledge learned in one task to improve performance in another related task. It helps in reducing the training time and improving sample efficiency.

Challenges in Reinforcement Learning

1. **Sample Efficiency**: RL algorithms often require a large number of interactions with the environment to learn effective policies, making them computationally expensive.
2. **Stability and Convergence**: Ensuring stable learning and convergence to optimal policies can be challenging, especially in environments with high-dimensional state and action spaces.
3. **Exploration in High-Dimensional Spaces**: Efficiently exploring large state and action spaces to discover rewarding actions is a significant challenge.
4. **Sparse Rewards**: In many real-world scenarios, rewards are sparse and delayed, making it difficult for the agent to learn the correlation between actions and outcomes.

Applications of Reinforcement Learning

Reinforcement learning has a wide range of applications across various domains, demonstrating its versatility and potential to solve complex problems.

1. **Robotics**: Training robots for tasks such as assembly, object manipulation, and navigation in dynamic environments.
2. **Finance**: Portfolio management, algorithmic trading, and risk management by learning optimal strategies through market interactions.

3. **Healthcare**: Personalized treatment planning, drug discovery, and optimizing clinical trials by learning from patient data.
4. **Energy Management**: Optimizing energy consumption in smart grids and buildings by learning from usage patterns and environmental conditions.
5. **Natural Language Processing**: Dialogue systems, language translation, and text summarization by learning optimal responses and translations through interaction.
6. **Logistics**: Route planning, inventory management, and supply chain optimization by learning efficient strategies through simulations.

Training and Optimization

Training a machine learning model involves adjusting its parameters based on data to minimize a loss function. This process requires significant computational resources and can be optimized using various techniques.

1. **Gradient Descent**: An optimization algorithm that iteratively updates the model's parameters to minimize the loss function. Variants include stochastic gradient descent (SGD) and mini-batch gradient descent.
2. **Regularization**: Techniques such as L1 and L2 regularization add constraints to the loss function to prevent overfitting.
3. **Cross-Validation**: A technique used to evaluate the model's performance on different subsets of the data, helping to ensure that it generalizes well to unseen data.
4. **Hyperparameter Tuning**: The process of finding the best set of hyperparameters (e.g., learning rate, batch size) for the model. Techniques include grid search, random search, and Bayesian optimization.

Neural Networks

Neural networks are a type of machine learning model inspired by the structure and function of the human brain. They consist of layers of interconnected nodes (neurons) that process data and learn complex patterns.

Structure of Neural Networks

Neurons and Activation Functions: Neurons are the basic units of a neural network. Each neuron receives input, applies a weighted sum to these inputs, adds a bias term, and then passes the result through an activation function. Common activation functions include sigmoid, tanh, and ReLU (Rectified Linear Unit).

Layers of a Neural Network: Neural networks consist of an input layer, one or more hidden layers, and an output layer. The input layer receives the raw data, the hidden layers perform intermediate computations, and the output layer produces the final prediction.

Types of Neural Networks

Feedforward Neural Networks (FNNs): The simplest type of neural network, where data flows in one direction from input to output. They are used for tasks such as image and speech recognition.

Convolutional Neural Networks (CNNs): Designed for processing grid-like data, such as images. CNNs use convolutional layers to detect features like edges and textures.

Recurrent Neural Networks (RNNs): Designed for sequential data, such as time series or natural language. RNNs maintain a hidden state that captures information about previous inputs.

Transformer Models: Use self-attention mechanisms to process input sequences in parallel, making them highly efficient and effective. Notable examples include Gemini, GPT-4, and T5.

Training Neural Networks

Forward Propagation: The process of passing input data through the network to generate predictions.

Loss Function: Measures the difference between the network's predictions and the actual labels. Common loss functions include mean squared error (MSE) for regression and cross-entropy loss for classification.

Backpropagation: An algorithm used to calculate the gradients of the loss function with respect to the network's weights. It propagates the error backward through the network, enabling efficient computation of gradients and updating weights accordingly.

Optimization Algorithms

Gradient Descent: Iteratively updates the weights to minimize the loss function.

Momentum: An extension of gradient descent that accumulates an exponentially decaying moving average of past gradients to accelerate convergence.

Adaptive Learning Rate Methods: Techniques such as AdaGrad, RMSprop, and Adam adjust the learning rate for each parameter based on past gradients.

Regularization Techniques

L1 and L2 Regularization: Add constraints to the loss function to prevent overfitting by encouraging smaller weights.

Dropout: Randomly sets a fraction of the neurons to zero during training, preventing the network from relying too heavily on any single neuron.

Batch Normalization: Normalizes the inputs to each layer, reducing internal covariate shift and improving training stability.

Deep Learning Advancements

Deep learning, a subset of machine learning, has led to significant advancements in the field of AI. By leveraging neural networks with many layers (hence "deep"), deep learning models can learn complex representations from large amounts of data.

Convolutional Neural Networks (CNNs)

CNNs are particularly well-suited for image processing tasks. They consist of convolutional layers that apply filters to the input data, pooling layers that downsample the data, and fully connected layers that perform the final classification.

Convolutional Layers: These layers apply a set of filters to the input data, producing feature maps that highlight important patterns.

Pooling Layers: These layers reduce the spatial dimensions of the feature maps, making the network more computationally efficient.

Fully Connected Layers: These layers flatten the feature maps and pass them through a series of dense layers to produce the final output.

Recurrent Neural Networks (RNNs)

RNNs are designed for sequential data, such as time series or natural language. They maintain a hidden state that captures information about previous inputs, allowing them to model dependencies over time.

Hidden State: The hidden state is a memory that stores information from previous time steps.

Long Short-Term Memory (LSTM): LSTM networks address the vanishing gradient problem by using gates to control the flow of information.

Gated Recurrent Unit (GRU): GRUs are a simplified version of LSTMs that use fewer gates but still effectively capture long-term dependencies.

Transformer Models

Transformer models have revolutionized NLP by using self-attention mechanisms to process input sequences in parallel. This architecture enables transformers to handle long-range dependencies and large datasets efficiently.

Self-Attention Mechanism: Allows the model to weigh the importance of different input tokens when making predictions.

Encoder-Decoder Architecture: Commonly used for tasks such as translation, where the encoder processes the input sequence, and the decoder generates the output sequence.

Positional Encoding: Provides information about the relative positions of tokens, since transformers do not have a built-in notion of sequence order.

Machine learning and neural networks form the foundation of AI agents, enabling them to learn from data, make predictions, and improve over time. Understanding the various types of machine learning, neural network architectures, training processes, and optimization techniques is crucial for harnessing the full potential of these powerful tools. As advancements in deep learning continue to emerge, the capabilities of AI agents will expand, opening up new possibilities for applications across various domains.

Dive Deep: Natural Language Processing (NLP)

Natural Language Processing (NLP) is a field of artificial intelligence that focuses on the interaction between computers and humans through natural language. The goal of NLP is to enable machines to understand, interpret, and generate human language in a way that is both meaningful and useful. NLP encompasses a range of tasks, from simple text processing to complex language understanding and generation.

Historical Context of NLP

NLP has a rich history that predates the modern concept of artificial intelligence. The development of NLP can be traced back to the early days of computing and linguistics.

Early Beginnings: 1950s - 1960s

The origins of NLP can be traced back to the 1950s, when researchers began exploring the possibility of automating language translation. The Georgetown-IBM experiment in 1954 was one of the first successful demonstrations of machine translation. The experiment translated over sixty Russian sentences into English using a simple rule-based system.

During the same period, Noam Chomsky's work on generative grammar revolutionized the field of linguistics. Chomsky introduced the concept of transformational grammar, which provided a theoretical framework for understanding the structure of language. His work laid the foundation for the development of syntactic parsing algorithms in NLP.

In 1966, Joseph Weizenbaum developed ELIZA, one of the earliest examples of a natural language processing system. ELIZA simulated conversation by using pattern matching and substitution rules. Although limited in its capabilities, ELIZA demonstrated the potential for computers to interact with humans through natural language.

Rule-Based Systems: 1970s - 1980s

The 1970s and 1980s saw the development of rule-based systems for NLP. These systems relied on handcrafted rules and linguistic knowledge to process and analyze text. Examples include:

1. **SYSTRAN**: Developed in the 1970s, SYSTRAN is one of the earliest machine translation systems. It used a combination of syntactic and semantic rules to translate text between languages. SYSTRAN was used by organizations such as the U.S. Air Force and the European Commission.
2. **SHRDLU**: Developed by Terry Winograd in 1971, SHRDLU was an early natural language understanding system that interacted with users in a simulated blocks world environment. SHRDLU could understand and execute commands, answer questions, and engage in simple dialogues.
3. **LUNAR**: Developed in the 1970s, LUNAR was a natural language question-answering system designed to answer questions about lunar rock samples collected during the Apollo missions. It used a combination of syntactic parsing and semantic interpretation to understand and respond to queries.

While rule-based systems demonstrated the potential of NLP, they had significant limitations. Handcrafting rules was time-consuming and required extensive linguistic expertise. Additionally, these systems struggled with the ambiguity and variability of natural language, leading to brittle and error-prone performance.

Statistical Methods and Machine Learning: 1990s - 2000s

The 1990s marked a paradigm shift in NLP with the introduction of statistical methods and machine learning. Researchers began leveraging large corpora of text and statistical models to learn language patterns and structures.

1. **Hidden Markov Models (HMMs)**: HMMs were used for tasks such as part-of-speech tagging and named entity recognition. These models leveraged probabilistic transitions between states to predict linguistic features based on observed data.

2. **N-gram Models**: N-gram models are probabilistic models that predict the likelihood of a word based on its preceding n-1 words. N-gram models were widely used in language modeling and speech recognition.

3. **Latent Semantic Analysis (LSA)**: LSA is a technique used to analyze relationships between words and concepts in a large corpus of text. It uses singular value decomposition to identify patterns and extract meaningful representations of text.

The rise of the internet and the availability of large-scale text data further fueled the development of statistical NLP methods. Machine learning algorithms such as decision trees, support vector machines, and maximum entropy models were applied to various NLP tasks, including text classification, sentiment analysis, and machine translation.

The Deep Learning Revolution: 2010s - Present

The advent of deep learning in the 2010s brought significant advancements to NLP. Deep learning models, particularly neural networks, revolutionized the field by achieving state-of-the-art performance across various NLP tasks.

1. **Word Embeddings**: Word embeddings, such as Word2Vec and GloVe, represented words as dense vectors in a continuous vector space. These embeddings captured semantic relationships between words, enabling better performance in tasks such as text classification and machine translation.

2.   **Recurrent Neural Networks (RNNs)**: RNNs and their variants, such as Long Short-Term Memory (LSTM) networks and Gated Recurrent Units (GRUs), were used for sequence modeling tasks. RNNs could capture dependencies between words in a sequence, making them effective for tasks such as language modeling and machine translation.

3.   **Transformer Models**: Transformer models, introduced by Vaswani et al. in 2017, revolutionized NLP with their self-attention mechanisms. Transformers enabled parallel processing of input sequences, leading to significant improvements in tasks such as language translation, text generation, and question answering. Notable transformer-based models include GEMINI, GPT-4, and T5.

4.   **Pre-trained Language Models**: Pre-trained language models, such as GEMINI (Bidirectional Encoder Representations from Transformers) and GPT-4 (Generative Pre-trained Transformer 3), achieved remarkable performance by training on massive amounts of text data. These models could be fine-tuned for specific tasks, enabling high accuracy and flexibility.

Fundamental Techniques in NLP

NLP encompasses a wide range of techniques for processing and analyzing text. These techniques form the building blocks for various NLP applications.

Text Preprocessing

Text preprocessing involves transforming raw text data into a format suitable for analysis. Key preprocessing steps include:

1.   **Tokenization**: Tokenization is the process of breaking down text into individual words or phrases, known as tokens. Tokenization can be as simple as splitting text by spaces or as complex as using algorithms to handle language-specific rules.

2.   **Stemming and Lemmatization**: Stemming reduces words to their base or root form by removing suffixes, while lemmatization maps words to their dictionary form. These techniques help normalize text data, reducing variations and improving the accuracy of NLP models.

3.   **Stopword Removal**: Stopwords are common words, such as "the," "and," and "in," that carry little semantic meaning. Removing stopwords reduces the dimensionality of the text data and focuses on the more meaningful words.

4.   **Lowercasing**: Converting text to lowercase ensures uniformity and reduces the complexity of the data. This step is particularly important for languages with case distinctions.

5.   **Part-of-Speech Tagging**: Part-of-speech tagging assigns grammatical labels (e.g., noun, verb, adjective) to each word in a text. This information is useful for understanding the syntactic structure and meaning of sentences.

Text Representation

Text representation involves converting text data into numerical formats that can be processed by machine learning algorithms. Key techniques include:

1.   **Bag of Words (BoW)**: BoW represents text as a collection of words, disregarding word order and syntax. Each document is represented as a vector of word frequencies or binary indicators.

2.   **TF-IDF (Term Frequency-Inverse Document Frequency)**: TF-IDF is a weighted representation that reflects the importance of words in a document relative to a corpus. Words that appear frequently in a document but rarely in the corpus are given higher weights.

3.   **Word Embeddings**: Word embeddings represent words as dense vectors in a continuous vector space. Embeddings capture semantic relationships between words, allowing models to

generalize better. Common embedding techniques include Word2Vec, GloVe, and FastText.

4. **Contextualized Embeddings**: Contextualized embeddings, such as those produced by GEMINI and GPT-4, capture the meaning of words in context. These embeddings consider the surrounding words, enabling more accurate and nuanced representations.

Text Analysis

Text analysis involves extracting meaningful information from text data. Key techniques include:

1. **Sentiment Analysis**: Sentiment analysis determines the sentiment or emotion expressed in a piece of text. It is widely used in social media monitoring, customer feedback analysis, and market research.
2. **Named Entity Recognition (NER)**: NER identifies and classifies named entities, such as people, organizations, locations, and dates, in a text. NER is used in information extraction, document classification, and question answering.
3. **Text Classification**: Text classification assigns predefined categories or labels to text documents. It is used in applications such as spam detection, topic classification, and sentiment analysis.
4. **Topic Modeling**: Topic modeling identifies the underlying topics or themes in a collection of documents. Techniques such as Latent Dirichlet Allocation (LDA) and Non-negative Matrix Factorization (NMF) are commonly used for topic modeling.

Language Generation

Language generation involves creating human-like text based on a given input. Key techniques include:

1. **Rule-Based Approaches**: Rule-based approaches use predefined templates and rules to generate text. While simple and

controllable, these methods often produce rigid and repetitive outputs.

2.   **Statistical Approaches**: Statistical approaches, such as n-gram models and Markov chains, generate text based on the probabilities of word sequences. These methods can capture more natural language patterns but may still lack coherence.

3.   **Neural Network Approaches**: Neural network models, such as RNNs and transformers, have revolutionized language generation. These models can generate coherent, contextually relevant text by learning from large datasets. Transformer-based models like GPT-4 have set new benchmarks in language generation tasks.

Advancements in NLP

The field of NLP has seen significant advancements in recent years, driven by the development of deep learning models and the availability of large-scale text data.

Transformer Models

Transformer models have transformed NLP with their self-attention mechanisms and parallel processing capabilities. Key transformer models include:

1.   **BERT (Bidirectional Encoder Representations from Transformers)**: BERT is a pre-trained language model that uses a bidirectional transformer to capture context from both directions. BERT has achieved state-of-the-art performance in various NLP tasks, including question answering, named entity recognition, and text classification.

2.   **Gemini**: Gemini is a pre-trained language model developed by Google that uses a bidirectional transformer to capture context from both directions. Gemini has surpassed BERT in performance, achieving state-of-the-art results in various NLP tasks, including

question answering, named entity recognition, and text classification.

3.   **GPT-4 (Generative Pre-trained Transformer 4)**: GPT-4 is a large-scale language model with 175 billion parameters. It generates high-quality text based on a given prompt and can perform tasks such as translation, summarization, and text completion with minimal fine-tuning.

4.   **T5 (Text-To-Text Transfer Transformer)**: T5 is a unified framework for NLP tasks that converts every problem into a text-to-text format. T5 has demonstrated strong performance across a wide range of tasks by leveraging transfer learning and large-scale pre-training.

Pre-trained Language Models

Pre-trained language models have revolutionized NLP by providing powerful representations that can be fine-tuned for specific tasks. These models leverage massive amounts of text data to learn rich linguistic patterns and structures.

1.   **Fine-Tuning**: Fine-tuning involves training a pre-trained language model on a specific task with task-specific data. This approach allows models to achieve high performance with relatively small amounts of labeled data.

2.   **Transfer Learning**: Transfer learning enables models to leverage knowledge from one task to improve performance on another task. Pre-trained language models can be adapted to various domains and applications, making them highly versatile.

Zero-Shot and Few-Shot Learning

Zero-shot and few-shot learning techniques enable models to perform tasks with little or no task-specific training data. These techniques are particularly useful for tasks with limited labeled data.

1. **Zero-Shot Learning**: Zero-shot learning involves training models to generalize to new tasks without any task-specific data. Models rely on general knowledge and transfer learning to make predictions.

2. **Few-Shot Learning**: Few-shot learning involves training models with a small number of task-specific examples. Techniques such as meta-learning and prompt-based learning have shown promise in enabling few-shot learning capabilities.

Challenges in NLP

Despite significant advancements, NLP still faces several challenges that researchers and practitioners must address.

Ambiguity and Context

Natural language is inherently ambiguous and context-dependent. Words and phrases can have multiple meanings, and their interpretation often depends on the surrounding context. Addressing ambiguity and capturing contextual information remains a significant challenge in NLP.

Polysemy: Polysemy refers to words with multiple meanings. For example, the word "bank" can refer to a financial institution or the side of a river. Disambiguating polysemous words requires understanding the context in which they are used.

Contextual Understanding: Capturing long-range dependencies and contextual information is crucial for accurate language understanding. Models must consider the entire context of a sentence or document to make accurate predictions.

Bias and Fairness

NLP models can inadvertently learn and propagate biases present in the training data. Addressing bias and ensuring fairness in NLP systems is essential for ethical and equitable AI.

Bias in Training Data: Training data often contains biases related to gender, race, and other attributes. Models trained on biased data can produce biased predictions and reinforce existing inequalities.

Fairness in Predictions: Ensuring fairness in NLP systems involves developing techniques to mitigate bias and promote equitable outcomes. Techniques such as adversarial training, bias regularization, and fairness constraints are being explored to address these issues.

Resource Limitations

Training large-scale NLP models requires significant computational resources and large amounts of data. Resource limitations can hinder the development and deployment of NLP systems.

Computational Costs: Training deep learning models, especially large transformer models, requires substantial computational power and energy. Developing more efficient algorithms and hardware is essential to reduce these costs.

Data Scarcity: Obtaining labeled data for specific tasks and domains can be challenging. Techniques such as transfer learning, semi-supervised learning, and data augmentation are used to address data scarcity.

Automation and Robotics

Automation systems are integral to the functionality of AI agents, enabling them to perform tasks traditionally done by humans. These systems leverage various AI technologies to control processes, manage workflows, and optimize operations. Automation systems can be broadly categorized into robotic process automation (RPA), industrial automation, service automation, and autonomous systems.

Robotic Process Automation (RPA)

Robotic Process Automation (RPA) involves using AI agents to automate repetitive and rule-based tasks in business processes. RPA bots mimic human actions to perform tasks such as data entry, invoice processing, and customer support. RPA improves productivity and accuracy while freeing up human workers for more strategic tasks.

Components of RPA

Bot Creation: RPA bots are created using specialized software tools that allow users to define workflows and automate tasks without extensive programming knowledge. These tools often include drag-and-drop interfaces and pre-built templates.

Workflow Automation: RPA bots follow predefined workflows to perform tasks, such as data extraction, form filling, and report generation. These workflows can be customized to meet specific business needs.

Integration with Systems: RPA bots can integrate with various enterprise systems, such as Customer Relationship Management (CRM), Enterprise Resource Planning (ERP), and databases, to streamline processes and improve efficiency.

Advantages of RPA

Cost Reduction: RPA reduces operational costs by automating repetitive tasks, thereby minimizing the need for human intervention.

Increased Accuracy: RPA bots perform tasks with high precision, reducing errors and improving data quality.

Scalability: RPA systems can be easily scaled to handle increased workloads without significant additional costs.

Compliance and Auditability: RPA ensures compliance with regulations by maintaining detailed logs of all activities, facilitating audits and compliance checks.

Challenges in RPA

Complex Process Automation: While RPA excels at automating simple, repetitive tasks, it struggles with more complex processes that require cognitive abilities.

Maintenance and Updates: RPA systems require regular maintenance and updates to ensure they continue to function correctly as underlying systems change.

Initial Setup Costs: The initial setup and implementation of RPA systems can be costly and time-consuming.

Industrial Automation

Industrial automation involves using AI agents to control manufacturing processes, optimize production lines, and ensure quality control. This automation improves efficiency, reduces costs, and enhances product quality.

Key Technologies in Industrial Automation

Programmable Logic Controllers (PLCs): PLCs are specialized computers used to control industrial processes. They can be programmed to perform specific tasks, such as monitoring sensors, controlling machinery, and managing production lines.

Supervisory Control and Data Acquisition (SCADA): SCADA systems provide real-time monitoring and control of industrial processes. They collect data from sensors and equipment, allowing operators to make informed decisions and optimize operations.

Industrial Robots: Industrial robots are used for tasks such as assembly, welding, painting, and packaging. These robots can work with high precision and speed, improving productivity and product quality.

Computer Numerical Control (CNC) Machines: CNC machines use computer programming to control the movement of tools and machinery, enabling precise and repeatable manufacturing processes.

Applications of Industrial Automation

Manufacturing: Industrial automation is widely used in manufacturing to automate production lines, reduce labor costs, and improve product quality. Examples include automotive assembly lines, electronics manufacturing, and food processing.

Quality Control: Automated quality control systems use AI and machine vision to inspect products for defects, ensuring high standards of quality and consistency.

Supply Chain Management: Automation systems optimize supply chain processes, from inventory management to logistics and distribution, improving efficiency and reducing costs.

Predictive Maintenance: AI-powered predictive maintenance systems analyze data from sensors and machinery to predict equipment failures before they occur, reducing downtime and maintenance costs.

Challenges in Industrial Automation

High Initial Costs: Implementing industrial automation systems requires significant upfront investment in hardware, software, and infrastructure.

Integration Complexity: Integrating automation systems with existing processes and equipment can be complex and requires careful planning and execution.

Workforce Impact: Automation can lead to job displacement, particularly for low-skilled workers, necessitating retraining and workforce development programs.

Service Automation

Service automation involves using AI-powered robots to assist in healthcare, hospitality, and retail environments. These robots can perform tasks such as patient care, cleaning, and inventory management, improving service quality and efficiency.

Applications of Service Automation

Healthcare: Service robots assist healthcare professionals by performing tasks such as patient monitoring, medication dispensing, and surgical assistance. These robots can improve patient outcomes and reduce the workload on healthcare staff.

Hospitality: In the hospitality industry, service robots are used for tasks such as room service, cleaning, and guest assistance. These robots enhance the guest experience by providing efficient and personalized services.

Retail: Service robots in retail environments help with inventory management, customer assistance, and checkout processes. These robots can improve operational efficiency and enhance the shopping experience for customers.

Advantages of Service Automation

Improved Efficiency: Service robots can perform tasks quickly and accurately, improving overall efficiency and productivity.

Enhanced Customer Experience: Service robots provide personalized and consistent service, enhancing customer satisfaction and loyalty.

Cost Savings: Automating routine tasks reduces labor costs and allows human workers to focus on more value-added activities.

Challenges in Service Automation

Technical Limitations: Service robots may have limitations in handling complex or unstructured environments, requiring ongoing advancements in AI and robotics technology.

High Costs: The development and deployment of service robots can be expensive, particularly for smaller businesses.

Human-Robot Interaction: Ensuring smooth and intuitive interactions between humans and robots is crucial for the success of service automation.

Autonomous Systems

Autonomous systems, such as self-driving cars and drones, leverage AI agents to navigate and operate independently. These technologies have applications in transportation, logistics, agriculture, and defense.

Key Components of Autonomous Systems

Perception: Autonomous systems use sensors, such as cameras, LiDAR, and radar, to perceive their environment. AI algorithms process this sensor data to detect objects, recognize patterns, and understand the environment.

Localization and Mapping: Autonomous systems use techniques like Simultaneous Localization and Mapping (SLAM) to create maps of their environment and determine their position within these maps. This information is crucial for navigation and path planning.

Decision Making: AI agents in autonomous systems make decisions based on sensor data and environmental maps. These decisions include route planning, obstacle avoidance, and task execution.

Control and Actuation: Autonomous systems use control algorithms to execute decisions and control actuators, such as motors and steering mechanisms. These algorithms ensure smooth and safe operation.

Applications of Autonomous Systems

Transportation: Autonomous vehicles, such as Tesla with FSD (Full Self-Driving Capability), are being developed for passenger transport, logistics, and public transit. These vehicles aim to improve safety, reduce traffic congestion, and increase transportation efficiency.

Agriculture: Autonomous drones and tractors are used for precision farming, including tasks such as planting, spraying, and harvesting. These technologies improve crop yields and reduce resource usage.

Logistics and Delivery: Autonomous robots and drones are used for last-mile delivery, warehouse automation, and inventory management, improving efficiency and reducing costs.

Defense: Autonomous systems are used in defense applications for surveillance, reconnaissance, and unmanned combat operations, enhancing operational capabilities and reducing risks to human personnel.

Challenges in Autonomous Systems

Safety and Reliability: Ensuring the safety and reliability of autonomous systems is paramount, particularly in high-stakes applications like transportation and defense.

Regulatory and Ethical Issues: The deployment of autonomous systems raises regulatory and ethical questions, including liability in case of accidents and the impact on employment.

Technical Complexity: Developing and deploying autonomous systems requires advanced AI algorithms, robust sensor technology, and extensive testing and validation.

Summary

In this chapter, we have explored the core technologies behind AI agents, including machine learning, neural networks, natural language processing, and automation systems. Understanding these technologies provides a foundation for comprehending how AI agents work and their potential applications.

As we delve deeper into the technical foundations, business applications, and personal impacts of AI agents in the following chapters, this knowledge will equip you with the tools to leverage AI effectively and responsibly.

Chapter 4: Types of AI Agents

AI agents are systems that perceive their environment through sensors and act upon that environment through actuators to achieve specific goals. The design and capabilities of these agents can vary significantly, leading to different classifications based on their complexity, learning ability, and autonomy. This chapter delves into the various types of AI agents, exploring their characteristics, functionalities, and applications.

Simple Reflex Agents

Simple reflex agents operate based on a set of predefined rules that map conditions to actions. They do not consider the history of percepts or the future consequences of their actions. These agents are reactive and only respond to the current state of the environment.

Characteristics

1. **Rule-Based**: Actions are triggered by specific conditions.
2. **Stateless**: They do not store past percepts or actions.
3. **Reactive**: Immediate response to environmental changes.

Example and Applications

Thermostats: Simple reflex agents that turn heating or cooling systems on or off based on the current temperature.

Automatic Doors: Open or close based on the presence of an object detected by sensors.

Model-Based Reflex Agents

Model-based reflex agents improve upon simple reflex agents by maintaining an internal state that tracks aspects of the environment that are not immediately observable. This internal state helps the agent make more informed decisions.

Characteristics

1. **Internal State**: Maintains a model of the world to handle partial observability.
2. **Improved Decision-Making**: Uses the internal state to make better decisions.
3. **Historical Context**: Considers past percepts to infer the current state.

Example and Applications

Robots with Obstacle Avoidance: Use sensors to detect obstacles and maintain an internal map of the environment to navigate safely.

Autonomous Vehicles: Track the state of the environment, including other vehicles and pedestrians, to make driving decisions.

Goal-Based Agents

Goal-based agents use goals to guide their actions. Unlike reflex agents, which only react to the current state, goal-based agents consider future states and plan their actions to achieve specific goals.

Characteristics

1. **Goal-Driven**: Actions are chosen to achieve specified goals.
2. **Planning**: Considers future consequences of actions.
3. **Flexible**: Can adapt to different situations by changing goals.

Example and Applications

Pathfinding Algorithms: Used in video games and robotics to find the shortest path to a destination.

Automated Planning Systems: Used in logistics to optimize delivery routes and schedules.

Utility-Based Agents

Utility-based agents extend goal-based agents by using a utility function to evaluate the desirability of different states. This allows them to handle trade-offs between competing goals and choose actions that maximize their overall utility.

Characteristics

1. **Utility Function**: Quantifies the desirability of different states.
2. **Optimization**: Chooses actions that maximize expected utility.
3. **Sophisticated Decision-Making**: Balances multiple objectives and constraints.

Example and Applications

Recommendation Systems: Suggest products or services based on user preferences and maximize user satisfaction.

Economic Agents: Make decisions based on utility functions representing profit, cost, and risk.

Learning Agents

Learning agents have the ability to learn from their experiences and improve their performance over time. They consist of four main components: the learning element, the performance element, the critic, and the problem generator.

Characteristics

1. **Adaptive**: Improve performance through learning.
2. **Feedback Loop**: Use feedback from the environment to guide learning.
3. **Exploration and Exploitation**: Balance between exploring new actions and exploiting known actions.

Example and Applications

Game Playing Agents: Learn strategies and improve their gameplay over time, such as AlphaGo.

Speech Recognition Systems: Improve accuracy by learning from user corrections.

Autonomous Agents

Autonomous agents operate independently, making decisions and taking actions without human intervention. They are capable of adapting to changes in the environment and achieving long-term goals.

Characteristics

1. **Independence**: Operate without human intervention.
2. **Adaptability**: Adjust to changes in the environment.

3. **Long-Term Goals**: Pursue objectives over extended periods.

Example and Applications

Self-Driving Cars: Navigate roads, obey traffic rules, and make driving decisions independently.

Personal Assistants: Perform tasks like scheduling, reminders, and information retrieval autonomously.

Multi-Agent Systems

Multi-agent systems consist of multiple interacting agents that can collaborate or compete to achieve their objectives. These systems are used to solve problems that are too complex for a single agent.

Characteristics

1. **Interaction**: Agents communicate and interact with each other.
2. **Collaboration and Competition**: Can work together or compete for resources.
3. **Distributed Problem Solving**: Solve complex problems through collective intelligence.

Example and Applications

Smart Grid Management: Multiple agents manage different aspects of the power grid to optimize energy distribution.

Collaborative Robotics: Teams of robots work together to accomplish tasks like warehouse automation.

Detailed Exploration of AI Agents

Simple Reflex Agents

Simple reflex agents are the most basic form of AI agents. They operate based on a set of predefined rules that map conditions (inputs) directly to actions (outputs). These agents do not have the capability to store past experiences or consider future consequences of their actions. Their behavior is entirely reactive, making them suitable for straightforward tasks where quick responses are necessary.

Example: Thermostats

Thermostats are classic examples of simple reflex agents. They monitor the current temperature and activate heating or cooling systems based on predefined thresholds. For instance, if the temperature drops below a certain point, the thermostat turns on the heater. Conversely, if the temperature rises above a set level, the cooling system is activated. This direct mapping of temperature conditions to actions ensures a quick and efficient response to maintain a desired temperature range.

Challenges and Limitations

Lack of Flexibility: Simple reflex agents cannot adapt to new situations beyond their predefined rules.

No Learning Capability: These agents cannot learn from their experiences or improve their performance over time.

Limited Scope: Suitable only for environments where all necessary actions can be predefined and do not require consideration of historical data or future planning.

Model-Based Reflex Agents

Model-based reflex agents extend the capabilities of simple reflex agents by maintaining an internal state that represents unobservable aspects of the current situation. This internal state is updated based on incoming percepts and a model of how the world works. By keeping track of the internal state, these agents can handle partially observable environments and make more informed decisions.

Example: Robots with Obstacle Avoidance

Consider a robot navigating a cluttered environment. A model-based reflex agent in the robot uses sensors to detect obstacles and maintains an internal map of the surroundings. As the robot moves, it updates this map and plans its path accordingly, avoiding obstacles and finding the most efficient route to its destination. This internal state allows the robot to navigate complex environments more effectively than a simple reflex agent.

Benefits and Applications

Enhanced Decision-Making: The internal state enables more informed decisions by considering the broader context.

Improved Performance: Better handling of partially observable environments, leading to more robust and reliable performance.

Applications: Widely used in robotics, autonomous vehicles, and any system requiring real-time decision-making in dynamic environments.

Goal-Based Agents

Goal-based agents are more sophisticated than reflex agents. They not only react to the environment but also act to achieve specific goals. These agents have a goal that they aim to achieve and use planning to decide on a sequence of actions that will lead them to that goal. By considering future states and outcomes, goal-based agents can handle more complex and dynamic environments.

Example: Pathfinding Algorithms

In video games and robotics, pathfinding algorithms are used to navigate characters or robots from one point to another. A goal-based agent determines the optimal path by considering various possible routes and selecting the one that leads to the destination most efficiently. Techniques like A* (A-star) algorithm are commonly used for this purpose, evaluating paths based on the cost to reach the goal.

Advantages

Future-Oriented: Considers future consequences and plans accordingly.

Flexibility: Can adapt to different goals by changing the objective.

Complex Problem Solving: Capable of solving more complex problems that require planning and foresight.

Utility-Based Agents

Utility-based agents extend goal-based agents by using a utility function to evaluate the desirability of different states. This allows them to handle trade-offs between competing goals and choose actions that maximize their overall utility. Utility functions provide a way to quantify preferences over different outcomes, enabling more nuanced decision-making.

Example: Recommendation Systems

Online recommendation systems, such as those used by Amazon or Netflix, aim to suggest products or content that maximizes user satisfaction. A utility-based agent in these systems evaluates various factors, such as user preferences, past behavior, and product ratings, to recommend items that are most likely to be enjoyed by the user. By optimizing the utility function, the system improves user experience and engagement.

Benefits

Optimized Decision-Making: Chooses actions that maximize overall utility.

Balanced Outcomes: Handles trade-offs between different objectives.

Sophisticated Reasoning: Provides a framework for more sophisticated and personalized decision-making.

Learning Agents

Learning agents have the ability to learn from their experiences and improve their performance over time. These agents consist of four main components: the learning element, the performance element, the critic, and the problem generator. The learning element makes improvements based on feedback, the performance element carries out actions, the critic provides feedback on performance, and the problem generator suggests new experiences to learn from. This ability to learn and adapt makes learning agents highly versatile and capable of handling complex, dynamic environments.

Components of Learning Agents

1. **Learning Element**: Responsible for making improvements to the agent's knowledge and behavior based on feedback from the critic.
2. **Performance Element**: Executes actions based on the current knowledge and strategy of the agent.
3. **Critic**: Evaluates the performance of the agent and provides feedback that the learning element uses to make adjustments.
4. **Problem Generator**: Suggests actions that will lead to new and informative experiences, aiding the learning process.

Types of Learning

1. **Supervised Learning**: The agent is trained on a labeled dataset where each input is paired with the correct output. The goal is to learn a mapping from inputs to outputs that can be generalized to new, unseen data.
2. **Unsupervised Learning**: The agent is trained on an unlabeled dataset and must identify patterns and structures within the data.
3. **Reinforcement Learning**: The agent learns by interacting with its environment, receiving rewards or penalties based on its actions. The goal is to maximize cumulative rewards over time.

Example: Game Playing Agents

AlphaGo, developed by DeepMind, is a prime example of a learning agent. AlphaGo was trained using a combination of supervised learning and reinforcement learning. Initially, it learned from a dataset of human expert games, and then it improved its performance by playing millions of games against itself. This approach allowed AlphaGo to develop strategies and tactics far beyond those of its human counterparts, ultimately defeating world champion Go players.

Performance and Critique: AlphaGo's performance element involves making moves based on its learned strategy, while the critic evaluates the outcome of each game, providing feedback that helps refine the strategy.

Applications

Game Playing: Learning agents are extensively used in developing AI for games. By learning from past games and simulating future scenarios, these agents can outperform human players in complex games such as Chess, Go, and Dota 2.

Speech Recognition: Systems like Apple's Siri, Amazon's Alexa, and Google Assistant continually improve their accuracy by learning from user interactions and corrections.

Autonomous Vehicles: Learning agents enable self-driving cars to adapt to new driving conditions, improving safety and efficiency over time.

Healthcare: AI systems learn from medical records to assist in diagnosing diseases, personalizing treatment plans, and predicting patient outcomes.

Advantages

Adaptability: Learning agents can adapt to changes in their environment and improve their performance over time.

Continuous Improvement: These agents can continuously refine their strategies and behaviors, leading to better performance and efficiency.

Versatility: Learning agents can be applied to a wide range of domains, from gaming to healthcare to autonomous systems.

Disadvantages

Complexity: Designing and training learning agents can be complex and resource-intensive.

Data Requirements: Effective learning often requires large amounts of data, which may not always be available.

Overfitting: There is a risk of the agent learning to perform well on the training data but failing to generalize to new, unseen data.

Autonomous Agents

Autonomous agents operate independently, making decisions and taking actions without human intervention. They are capable of adapting to changes in the environment and achieving long-term goals. Autonomous agents combine advanced decision-making capabilities with the ability to operate in dynamic, unpredictable environments.

Characteristics

Independence: Autonomous agents can function without human oversight.

Adaptability: These agents can adjust their strategies based on environmental changes.

Long-Term Goals: Autonomous agents are designed to pursue objectives over extended periods.

Examples and Applications

Self-Driving Cars: Autonomous vehicles navigate roads, obey traffic rules, and make driving decisions independently. Companies like Tesla, Waymo, and Uber are at the forefront of developing self-driving technologies.

Personal Assistants: Digital assistants like Siri, Alexa, and Google Assistant perform tasks such as scheduling, reminders, and information retrieval autonomously.

Autonomous Drones: Used in applications ranging from surveillance and environmental monitoring to package delivery and agricultural management.

Advantages

Independence: Reduce the need for constant human oversight, allowing for more efficient task execution.

Flexibility: Can handle a wide range of tasks and adapt to new challenges without requiring reprogramming.

Efficiency: Perform tasks continuously and accurately, often outperforming human counterparts.

Disadvantages

Complex Design: Developing autonomous agents requires advanced algorithms and significant computational power.

Ethical and Legal Issues: Raises questions about accountability and decision-making in critical situations.

Reliability: Ensuring consistent and safe performance in dynamic environments is challenging.

Collaborative Agents

Collaborative agents work together to achieve common goals. These agents communicate and coordinate with each other, making them suitable for tasks that require teamwork. Collaborative agents can be found in multi-agent systems where different agents bring various skills and resources to solve complex problems.

Characteristics

Communication: Share information with other agents to achieve common goals.

Coordination: Work together by distributing tasks and responsibilities.

Distributed Problem Solving: Solve complex problems through collective intelligence.

Examples and Applications

Multi-Agent Systems: Used in smart grids to optimize energy distribution by having multiple agents manage different aspects of the power grid.

Collaborative Robotics: Teams of robots working together in manufacturing and logistics to accomplish tasks more efficiently.

Swarm Intelligence: Inspired by natural systems like ant colonies and bird flocks, where simple agents follow simple rules to achieve complex behaviors.

Advantages

Scalability: Can handle large, complex problems by distributing tasks among multiple agents.

Robustness: Can adapt to changes and failures in individual agents, maintaining overall system performance.

Efficiency: Achieve goals more effectively through teamwork and collaboration.

Disadvantages

Complexity in Coordination: Requires sophisticated algorithms for communication and coordination among agents.

Resource Sharing: May face challenges in resource allocation and conflict resolution.

Latency: Communication delays can affect performance in real-time applications.

Chapter 5: AI Agents in Business Today

The business landscape is being transformed by the integration of AI agents. From enhancing customer service to optimizing operations, AI agents are driving innovation and efficiency across various industries. This chapter delves into the numerous ways AI agents are being utilized in business today, examining their impact, benefits, and the challenges they present.

Case Studies and Success Stories

Customer Service and Support

AI agents have revolutionized customer service by providing instant, accurate responses to customer queries. These agents, often in the form of chatbots or virtual assistants, can handle a wide range of tasks, from answering frequently asked questions to resolving complex issues.

Chatbots

Chatbots are one of the most common applications of AI agents in customer service. They are designed to simulate human conversation and can be integrated into websites, social media platforms, and messaging apps.

Characteristics

24/7 Availability: Chatbots can provide support around the clock, ensuring that customers receive assistance whenever they need it.

Instant Responses: Unlike human agents, chatbots can respond to multiple queries simultaneously, reducing wait times.

Consistency: Chatbots provide consistent responses, ensuring that all customers receive the same level of service.

Examples and Applications

E-commerce: Chatbots on e-commerce websites assist customers with product inquiries, order tracking, and return processes.

Banking: Financial institutions use chatbots to help customers with account management, transaction history, and fraud alerts.

Healthcare: Healthcare providers use chatbots to schedule appointments, provide medical information, and triage patients.

Benefits

Cost Reduction: Chatbots reduce the need for large customer support teams, leading to significant cost savings.

Scalability: Businesses can handle an increasing number of customer inquiries without the need to hire additional staff.

Enhanced Customer Experience: Instant responses and 24/7 availability improve overall customer satisfaction.

Virtual Assistants

Virtual assistants are more advanced than chatbots and are capable of performing a wider range of tasks. These AI agents can manage calendars, send reminders, and even make phone calls on behalf of users.

Characteristics

Voice Interaction: Virtual assistants often use voice recognition technology to interact with users.

Task Automation: They can automate repetitive tasks, such as scheduling meetings or setting reminders.

Personalization

Personalization involves using AI agents to tailor marketing messages and product recommendations to individual customers. This approach increases customer engagement and drives sales.

Characteristics

User Data: AI agents collect and analyze user data to understand preferences and behaviors.

Customized Content: Based on the analysis, these agents create personalized marketing messages and recommendations.

Real-Time Adaptation: AI agents can adjust personalization strategies in real-time based on user interactions.

Examples and Applications

E-commerce: Online retailers use personalization to recommend products based on browsing and purchase history.

Streaming Services: Platforms like Netflix and Spotify use AI agents to recommend movies, TV shows, and music based on user preferences.

Email Marketing: AI agents personalize email content and send targeted campaigns to increase engagement and conversion rates.

Benefits

Increased Engagement: Personalized content is more relevant to users, leading to higher engagement rates.

Higher Conversion Rates: Personalized recommendations are more likely to result in sales.

Customer Loyalty: Personalization enhances the customer experience, fostering loyalty and repeat business.

Operations and Supply Chain Management

AI agents are optimizing operations and supply chain management by improving efficiency, reducing costs, and minimizing disruptions.

Inventory Management

AI agents are used to optimize inventory levels, ensuring that businesses have the right amount of stock to meet customer demand without overstocking.

Characteristics

Demand Forecasting: AI agents analyze sales data to predict future demand.

Automated Reordering: Based on demand forecasts, AI agents can automatically reorder stock when levels fall below a certain threshold.

Inventory Optimization: These agents balance inventory levels to minimize holding costs while avoiding stockouts.

Examples and Applications

Retail: Retailers use AI agents to manage inventory across multiple locations, ensuring that popular products are always in stock.

Manufacturing: Manufacturers use AI agents to optimize the supply of raw materials and components.

E-commerce: E-commerce platforms use AI agents to manage warehouse inventory and streamline order fulfillment.

Benefits

Reduced Costs: Optimized inventory levels reduce holding costs and minimize waste.

Improved Efficiency: Automated reordering and inventory optimization streamline operations.

Enhanced Customer Satisfaction: Ensuring that products are always in stock improves customer satisfaction and loyalty.

Logistics and Transportation

AI agents are enhancing logistics and transportation by optimizing routes, predicting maintenance needs, and improving fleet management.

Characteristics

Route Optimization: AI agents analyze traffic data and delivery schedules to determine the most efficient routes.

Predictive Maintenance: These agents predict when vehicles will need maintenance, reducing downtime and preventing breakdowns.

Fleet Management: AI agents monitor and manage fleets, ensuring optimal performance and utilization.

Examples and Applications

Delivery Services: Companies like UPS and FedEx use AI agents to optimize delivery routes and schedules.

Public Transportation: AI agents help public transportation systems optimize routes and schedules, improving service reliability.

Ride-Sharing: Platforms like Uber and Lyft use AI agents to match drivers with passengers and optimize routes.

Benefits

Cost Savings: Route optimization and predictive maintenance reduce operational costs.

Improved Efficiency: AI agents streamline logistics and transportation processes, enhancing overall efficiency.

Increased Reliability: Predictive maintenance and fleet management improve the reliability of transportation services.

Finance and Accounting

AI agents are transforming finance and accounting by automating processes, enhancing fraud detection, and providing financial insights.

Automated Accounting

AI agents are used to automate routine accounting tasks, such as bookkeeping, invoicing, and payroll processing.

Characteristics

Data Entry Automation: AI agents automatically enter and categorize financial data.

Reconciliation: These agents reconcile accounts, ensuring that financial records are accurate and up-to-date.

Compliance: AI agents ensure that financial processes comply with regulations and standards.

Examples and Applications

Small Businesses: AI-powered accounting software helps small businesses manage their finances efficiently.

Corporate Finance: Large organizations use AI agents to automate complex accounting processes and ensure compliance.

Tax Preparation: AI agents assist in preparing and filing tax returns, ensuring accuracy and compliance.

Benefits

Time Savings: Automating routine tasks frees up time for finance professionals to focus on strategic activities.

Accuracy: AI agents reduce the risk of human error, ensuring accurate financial records.

Cost Reduction: Automation reduces the need for manual labor, leading to cost savings.

Fraud Detection

AI agents enhance fraud detection by analyzing transaction data and identifying suspicious activities.

Characteristics

Anomaly Detection: AI agents detect unusual patterns and behaviors that may indicate fraud.

Real-Time Monitoring: These agents continuously monitor transactions, providing real-time alerts for suspicious activities.

Risk Assessment: AI agents assess the risk of transactions and flag high-risk activities for further investigation.

Examples and Applications

Banking: Financial institutions use AI agents to monitor transactions and detect fraudulent activities.

E-commerce: E-commerce platforms use AI agents to identify and prevent fraudulent transactions.

Insurance: Insurance companies use AI agents to detect fraudulent claims and prevent losses.

Benefits

Increased Security: AI agents enhance the security of financial transactions by detecting and preventing fraud.

Cost Savings: Preventing fraud reduces financial losses and associated costs.

Improved Compliance: AI agents help businesses comply with regulations by monitoring and reporting suspicious activities.

Financial Insights

AI agents provide financial insights by analyzing data and generating reports, helping businesses make informed decisions.

Characteristics

Data Analysis: AI agents analyze financial data to identify trends and patterns.

Reporting: These agents generate financial reports, providing insights into business performance.

Forecasting: AI agents predict future financial performance based on historical data.

Examples and Applications

Financial Planning: Businesses use AI agents to create financial plans and forecasts.

Investment Management: AI agents assist in portfolio management by analyzing market trends and predicting investment performance.

Budgeting: AI agents help businesses create and manage budgets, ensuring financial stability.

Benefits

Informed Decision-Making: AI agents provide valuable insights, enabling businesses to make informed financial decisions.

Improved Efficiency: Automated data analysis and reporting streamline financial processes.

Enhanced Performance: By predicting future performance, AI agents help businesses optimize their financial strategies.

Human Resources and Talent Management

AI agents are transforming human resources and talent management by automating processes, enhancing recruitment, and improving employee engagement.

Recruitment

AI agents streamline the recruitment process by automating candidate screening, shortlisting, and interview scheduling.

Characteristics

Resume Screening: AI agents analyze resumes and identify the most qualified candidates.

Candidate Shortlisting: These agents create shortlists based on predefined criteria, ensuring that only the best candidates are considered.

Interview Scheduling: AI agents schedule interviews, coordinating between candidates and hiring managers.

Examples and Applications

Job Portals: Platforms like LinkedIn use AI agents to match candidates with job openings based on their profiles and skills.

Recruitment Agencies: Agencies use AI agents to screen and shortlist candidates, speeding up the hiring process.

Corporate HR: Large organizations use AI agents to manage recruitment, ensuring a smooth and efficient hiring process.

Benefits

Time Savings: Automating recruitment tasks reduces the time and effort required to hire new employees.

Improved Candidate Quality: AI agents ensure that only the most qualified candidates are considered, improving the quality of hires.

Efficiency: Streamlining the recruitment process enhances overall efficiency and reduces the time-to-hire.

Employee Engagement

AI agents improve employee engagement by providing personalized recommendations, managing feedback, and facilitating communication.

Characteristics

Personalized Recommendations: AI agents provide personalized recommendations for training, career development, and wellness programs.

Feedback Management: These agents collect and analyze employee feedback, providing insights into employee satisfaction and engagement.

Communication Facilitation: AI agents facilitate communication between employees and management, ensuring that concerns are addressed promptly.

Examples and Applications

Corporate Training: AI agents recommend training programs based on employee skills and career goals.

Employee Surveys: AI agents analyze survey data to identify trends and areas for improvement in employee satisfaction.

Internal Communication: AI-powered chatbots facilitate communication by answering employee queries and providing information.

Benefits

Increased Engagement: Personalized recommendations and effective feedback management improve employee engagement.

Enhanced Satisfaction: Addressing employee concerns promptly enhances overall job satisfaction.

Improved Retention: Engaged and satisfied employees are more likely to stay with the company, reducing turnover rates.

Key Industries Benefiting from AI Agents

AI agents are making a significant impact across various industries, driving innovation, improving efficiency, and enhancing customer experiences. This section explores some of the key industries that are reaping the benefits of AI agents, providing detailed insights into how these intelligent systems are being utilized to transform business operations and deliver value.

Healthcare

The healthcare industry has seen substantial advancements through the integration of AI agents. These systems are enhancing patient care, streamlining administrative processes, and driving medical research forward.

Patient Care

AI agents are revolutionizing patient care by providing personalized treatment plans, improving diagnostic accuracy, and facilitating remote monitoring.

Personalized Treatment Plans: AI agents analyze patient data, including medical history, genetic information, and lifestyle factors, to create customized treatment plans. This personalized approach improves treatment outcomes and enhances patient satisfaction.

Diagnostic Accuracy: AI-powered diagnostic tools assist healthcare professionals in identifying diseases and conditions with high accuracy. For instance, AI agents can analyze medical images to detect tumors or predict the likelihood of certain diseases based on patient data.

Remote Monitoring: AI agents enable remote monitoring of patients with chronic conditions, allowing healthcare providers to track vital signs and detect potential issues early. This continuous monitoring reduces hospital readmissions and improves patient outcomes.

Administrative Efficiency

AI agents streamline administrative tasks, reducing the burden on healthcare professionals and improving operational efficiency.

Appointment Scheduling: AI agents manage appointment scheduling, ensuring that patients are booked efficiently and minimizing no-show rates.

Billing and Claims Processing: AI systems automate billing and claims processing, reducing errors and speeding up reimbursement processes.

Patient Records Management: AI agents organize and manage patient records, making it easier for healthcare providers to access and update information.

Medical Research

AI agents are accelerating medical research by analyzing large datasets, identifying patterns, and predicting outcomes.

1. **Drug Discovery**: AI agents assist in drug discovery by analyzing chemical compounds and predicting their efficacy in treating diseases. This accelerates the development of new medications and reduces research costs.
2. **Clinical Trials**: AI systems identify suitable candidates for clinical trials and predict their potential outcomes, improving the efficiency of trial processes.
3. **Genomic Research**: AI agents analyze genomic data to identify genetic markers associated with diseases, advancing our understanding of genetics and enabling personalized medicine.

Retail

The retail industry is leveraging AI agents to enhance customer experiences, optimize inventory management, and drive sales.

Customer Experience

AI agents improve customer experiences by providing personalized recommendations, enhancing customer service, and facilitating seamless shopping experiences.

1. **Personalized Recommendations**: AI agents analyze customer behavior and preferences to provide personalized product recommendations. This increases customer satisfaction and drives sales.
2. **Enhanced Customer Service**: Chatbots and virtual assistants handle customer inquiries, process returns, and provide support, ensuring a smooth shopping experience.
3. **Seamless Shopping Experiences**: AI agents enable features such as voice-activated shopping, virtual try-ons, and augmented reality experiences, making shopping more convenient and engaging.

Inventory Management

AI agents optimize inventory management by predicting demand, automating restocking processes, and reducing waste.

1. **Demand Prediction**: AI agents analyze sales data and market trends to predict future demand, ensuring that retailers stock the right products at the right time.
2. **Automated Restocking**: These systems automate the restocking process, reducing the likelihood of stockouts and overstocking.

3. **Waste Reduction**: By optimizing inventory levels, AI agents help retailers reduce waste and improve sustainability.

Sales and Marketing

AI agents drive sales and marketing efforts by providing deep insights into customer behavior, optimizing marketing campaigns, and enhancing targeting strategies.

1. **Customer Insights**: AI agents analyze customer data to provide insights into shopping behavior, preferences, and trends. This information helps retailers tailor their offerings and marketing strategies.
2. **Campaign Optimization**: AI-powered marketing tools optimize campaigns by predicting their effectiveness and adjusting strategies in real-time.
3. **Targeted Marketing**: AI agents enhance targeting strategies by identifying the most promising customer segments and delivering personalized marketing messages.

Finance

The finance industry is experiencing significant transformations through the adoption of AI agents, particularly in areas such as fraud detection, investment management, and customer service.

1. **Fraud Detection**
2. AI agents enhance fraud detection by analyzing transaction data, identifying suspicious activities, and preventing fraudulent transactions.
3. **Anomaly Detection**: AI agents detect unusual patterns and behaviors in transaction data, flagging potential fraud.
4. **Real-Time Monitoring**: These systems continuously monitor transactions, providing real-time alerts for suspicious activities.

5. **Risk Assessment**: AI agents assess the risk of transactions and flag high-risk activities for further investigation.

Investment Management

AI agents assist in investment management by analyzing market trends, predicting asset performance, and optimizing portfolios.

1. **Market Analysis**: AI agents analyze market data to identify trends and predict future movements, helping investors make informed decisions.
2. **Portfolio Optimization**: These systems optimize investment portfolios by balancing risk and return based on investor preferences.
3. **Automated Trading**: AI agents execute trades automatically based on predefined strategies, improving trading efficiency and reducing costs.

Customer Service

AI agents improve customer service in the finance industry by providing instant support, personalized recommendations, and efficient problem resolution.

1. **Virtual Assistants**: AI-powered virtual assistants handle customer inquiries, manage account information, and provide financial advice.
2. **Personalized Recommendations**: AI agents analyze customer data to provide personalized financial products and services, enhancing customer satisfaction.
3. **Efficient Problem Resolution**: AI agents resolve customer issues quickly and accurately, reducing the need for human intervention.

Manufacturing

AI agents are driving innovation in the manufacturing industry by optimizing production processes, enhancing quality control, and improving supply chain management.

Production Optimization

AI agents optimize production processes by analyzing data, predicting maintenance needs, and improving efficiency.

1. **Predictive Maintenance**: AI agents predict when equipment will need maintenance, reducing downtime and preventing breakdowns.
2. **Process Optimization**: These systems analyze production data to identify inefficiencies and suggest improvements.
3. **Energy Management**: AI agents optimize energy usage in manufacturing facilities, reducing costs and environmental impact.

Quality Control

AI agents enhance quality control by inspecting products, identifying defects, and ensuring compliance with standards.

1. **Automated Inspection**: AI-powered vision systems inspect products for defects, ensuring high quality and consistency.
2. **Defect Detection**: These systems identify defects in real-time, allowing for immediate corrective actions.
3. **Standards Compliance**: AI agents ensure that products meet industry standards and regulatory requirements.

Supply Chain Management

AI agents improve supply chain management by optimizing logistics, managing inventory, and reducing disruptions.

1. **Logistics Optimization**: AI agents analyze logistics data to optimize transportation routes and schedules.
2. **Inventory Management**: These systems manage inventory levels, ensuring that materials and products are available when needed.
3. **Disruption Management**: AI agents predict potential disruptions in the supply chain and suggest mitigation strategies.

Transportation and Logistics

The transportation and logistics industry is leveraging AI agents to improve efficiency, enhance safety, and provide better services.

Fleet Management

AI agents optimize fleet management by monitoring vehicle performance, predicting maintenance needs, and improving route planning.

1. **Performance Monitoring**: AI agents monitor vehicle performance in real-time, ensuring optimal operation.
2. **Predictive Maintenance**: These systems predict maintenance needs, reducing downtime and preventing breakdowns.
3. **Route Planning**: AI agents optimize routes based on traffic data and delivery schedules, improving efficiency and reducing costs.

Autonomous Vehicles

AI agents are at the core of autonomous vehicle technology, enabling self-driving cars, trucks, and drones to operate safely and efficiently.

1. **Self-Driving Cars**: AI-powered systems navigate roads, obey traffic rules, and make driving decisions independently.
2. **Autonomous Trucks**: These vehicles transport goods over long distances without human intervention, improving efficiency and reducing costs.
3. **Delivery Drones**: AI agents control delivery drones, enabling fast and efficient parcel delivery.

Logistics Optimization

AI agents enhance logistics operations by optimizing warehouse management, improving inventory control, and reducing delivery times.

1. **Warehouse Management**: AI agents manage warehouse operations, ensuring efficient storage and retrieval of goods.
2. **Inventory Control**: These systems optimize inventory levels, reducing holding costs and preventing stockouts.
3. **Delivery Optimization**: AI agents optimize delivery schedules and routes, reducing delivery times and costs.

Energy

The energy industry is utilizing AI agents to optimize energy production, enhance grid management, and improve sustainability.

Energy Production

AI agents optimize energy production by predicting demand, managing resources, and improving efficiency.

1. **Demand Prediction**: AI agents analyze consumption data to predict future energy demand, ensuring optimal production levels.

2. **Resource Management**: These systems manage energy resources, balancing supply and demand to prevent shortages and surpluses.
3. **Efficiency Improvement**: AI agents optimize energy production processes, reducing costs and environmental impact.

Grid Management

AI agents enhance grid management by monitoring grid performance, predicting faults, and improving reliability.

1. **Performance Monitoring**: AI agents monitor grid performance in real-time, ensuring stable and reliable operation.
2. **Fault Prediction**: These systems predict potential faults in the grid, allowing for preventive maintenance and reducing downtime.
3. **Reliability Improvement**: AI agents optimize grid operations, improving overall reliability and reducing outages.

Sustainability

AI agents contribute to sustainability efforts by optimizing energy usage, reducing emissions, and supporting renewable energy integration.

1. **Energy Optimization**: AI agents optimize energy usage in buildings and industrial processes, reducing consumption and emissions.
2. **Emission Reduction**: These systems identify opportunities to reduce emissions, supporting environmental sustainability.

3. **Renewable Energy Integration**: AI agents manage the integration of renewable energy sources into the grid, ensuring stable and reliable supply.

Summary

The integration of AI agents across various industries is driving significant advancements and transforming business operations. These intelligent systems are revolutionizing the way organizations function, optimizing processes, enhancing customer experiences, and delivering substantial value. From healthcare to retail, finance to manufacturing, transportation to energy, AI agents are at the forefront of innovation, making a profound impact.

In healthcare, AI agents are providing personalized treatment plans, improving diagnostic accuracy, and facilitating remote patient monitoring. Retailers are leveraging AI to offer personalized recommendations, streamline inventory management, and enhance customer service. The finance industry benefits from AI through advanced fraud detection, investment management, and automated customer support. Manufacturing sees increased efficiency and reduced downtime with predictive maintenance and process optimization, while the transportation and logistics sector uses AI for route planning, fleet management, and autonomous vehicles. The energy industry is optimizing production, enhancing grid management, and supporting sustainability efforts through AI integration.

As AI technology continues to evolve, the potential applications and benefits of AI agents will only expand, offering new opportunities for businesses to thrive. These agents are driving efficiency, reducing costs, and enhancing both customer and employee experiences. By adopting and integrating AI technologies, businesses can stay competitive, optimize their processes, and deliver exceptional value to their customers and stakeholders.

The transformative potential of AI agents cannot be overstated. They are not only revolutionizing industries but also paving the way for a future where intelligent systems are at the core of business operations. As we continue to explore the myriad ways AI agents can be utilized, it becomes clear that their role in driving innovation and efficiency will only grow. Embracing the power of AI agents allows businesses to stay ahead of the competition and capitalize on the opportunities presented by this rapidly advancing technology.

In summary, AI agents are set to be a cornerstone of modern business, driving significant advancements across various sectors. Their ability to learn, adapt, and optimize makes them invaluable assets in today's competitive landscape. By leveraging AI agents, businesses can ensure they remain at the cutting edge of innovation, delivering unparalleled value and transforming the way they operate. The future of business is undoubtedly intertwined with the evolution of AI agents, promising a landscape of endless possibilities and continuous improvement.

Chapter 6: Building AI-Powered Products

Integrating AI into Existing Products

Integrating AI into existing products is a transformative process that can enhance functionality, improve user experience, and provide a competitive edge. This section explores the strategic considerations, technical requirements, and practical steps involved in incorporating AI into current products.

Strategic Considerations

Before diving into the technical aspects, it's essential to outline a clear strategy for integrating AI into existing products. This strategy should align with the company's overall business goals and address specific pain points or opportunities for improvement.

1. **Identify Objectives**: Determine the primary goals for integrating AI. These could include enhancing product features, improving user engagement, automating repetitive tasks, or gaining deeper insights from data.
2. **Assess Feasibility**: Evaluate the feasibility of AI integration by considering factors such as technical capabilities, available data, budget, and timeline. Conduct a thorough assessment to ensure that the proposed AI solution is viable and sustainable.
3. **Define Success Metrics**: Establish clear metrics to measure the success of the AI integration. These could include user adoption rates, performance improvements, cost savings, or revenue growth. Defining these metrics upfront helps track progress and demonstrate the value of the AI enhancements.
4. **Stakeholder Alignment**: Ensure that all stakeholders, including management, product teams, and end-users, are aligned with the AI integration strategy. Regular communication and collaboration are crucial to gaining buy-in and addressing any concerns or challenges.

Technical Requirements

Integrating AI into existing products requires a robust technical foundation. This includes data infrastructure, model development, and integration frameworks.

1. **Data Infrastructure**: A reliable data infrastructure is the backbone of any AI initiative. Ensure that the necessary data is collected, stored, and processed efficiently. This may involve setting up data pipelines, databases, and data warehouses to handle large volumes of information.
2. **Data Quality and Preprocessing**: High-quality data is critical for training effective AI models. Implement data cleaning and preprocessing steps to remove inconsistencies, handle missing values, and standardize formats. This improves the accuracy and reliability of AI predictions.
3. **Model Development**: Developing AI models involves selecting the appropriate algorithms, training them on relevant data, and fine-tuning their performance. Depending on the complexity of the task, this may require expertise in machine learning, deep learning, natural language processing, or computer vision.
4. **Integration Frameworks**: Choose integration frameworks and APIs that facilitate seamless interaction between the AI models and existing product features. Popular frameworks like TensorFlow, PyTorch, and scikit-learn offer robust tools for building and deploying AI models.

Practical Steps for AI Integration

Integrating AI into existing products involves a series of practical steps, from initial planning to deployment and continuous improvement.

1. **Proof of Concept (PoC)**: Start with a PoC to validate the feasibility and potential impact of the AI integration. This involves

developing a prototype that demonstrates how AI can enhance specific product features. Gather feedback from stakeholders and refine the approach based on their input.

2. **Data Collection and Preparation**: Collect and prepare the data needed for training AI models. This may involve aggregating historical data, generating synthetic data, or conducting experiments to gather new data. Ensure that the data is representative of real-world scenarios and covers a wide range of use cases.

3. **Model Training and Evaluation**: Train AI models using the prepared data and evaluate their performance against predefined metrics. This may involve iterative cycles of training, testing, and refinement to achieve the desired level of accuracy and reliability.

4. **Integration and Testing**: Integrate the trained AI models into the existing product architecture. This involves developing APIs, user interfaces, and backend systems to enable seamless interaction between the AI components and other product features. Conduct thorough testing to identify and resolve any issues.

5. **Deployment and Monitoring**: Deploy the AI-enhanced product to production environments and monitor its performance. Implement monitoring tools to track key metrics, detect anomalies, and gather user feedback. This helps identify areas for improvement and ensures that the AI components continue to perform as expected.

6. **Continuous Improvement**: AI integration is an ongoing process that requires continuous improvement. Collect and analyze user feedback, monitor performance metrics, and update models as needed. This iterative approach ensures that the AI-enhanced product remains relevant and effective over time.

Case Study 1: AI Integration in E-commerce

To illustrate the practical steps and benefits of AI integration, let's consider a case study of an e-commerce platform that incorporates AI to enhance product recommendations and customer service.

Objective

The e-commerce platform aims to improve user engagement and sales by providing personalized product recommendations and efficient customer service.

Data Infrastructure

The platform sets up a data warehouse to store user interaction data, purchase history, and product information. Data pipelines are established to collect real-time data from user activities and transactions.

Data Preparation

Data scientists clean and preprocess the data to remove duplicates, handle missing values, and standardize formats. They create features such as user preferences, browsing patterns, and purchase behaviors.

Model Development

Machine learning models are developed to predict user preferences and recommend products. Collaborative filtering and content-based filtering algorithms are used to generate personalized recommendations. Additionally, natural language processing models are trained to handle customer service queries through chatbots.

Integration and Testing

The AI models are integrated into the e-commerce platform using APIs. The recommendation engine is embedded in the product pages, and the chatbot is integrated into the customer service interface. Extensive testing is conducted to ensure seamless interaction and accurate responses.

Deployment and Monitoring

The AI-enhanced platform is deployed to production. Monitoring tools track user engagement, recommendation accuracy, and chatbot performance. User feedback is collected to identify areas for improvement.

Continuous Improvement

Based on user feedback and performance metrics, the AI models are periodically retrained and updated. New features are added to enhance the recommendation engine, and the chatbot is continuously improved to handle a wider range of queries.

Challenges and Solutions

Integrating AI into existing products comes with its set of challenges. Understanding these challenges and implementing effective solutions is crucial for successful AI integration.

1.   **Data Privacy and Security**: Ensuring data privacy and security is paramount when integrating AI. Implement robust encryption, access controls, and compliance with regulations such as GDPR to protect user data.
2.   **Scalability**: AI models need to scale efficiently to handle increasing volumes of data and user interactions. Use cloud-based solutions and distributed computing frameworks to ensure scalability.
3.   **User Adoption**: Gaining user trust and encouraging adoption of AI-enhanced features can be challenging. Provide clear explanations of AI functionalities, offer user training, and gather feedback to improve user experience.
4.   **Bias and Fairness**: AI models can inadvertently introduce bias into decision-making processes. Implement fairness metrics, conduct regular audits, and use diverse training data to mitigate bias.

5.   **Maintenance and Updates**: AI models require regular maintenance and updates to remain effective. Establish a process for continuous monitoring, retraining, and updating models based on new data and changing requirements.

Case Study 2: AI Integration in Healthcare

To further illustrate the versatility and impact of AI integration, let's explore a case study in the healthcare industry. This case study demonstrates how AI can be leveraged to improve patient care, streamline administrative tasks, and support medical research.

Objective

A healthcare provider aims to enhance patient outcomes and operational efficiency by integrating AI into patient monitoring and administrative processes.

Data Infrastructure

The healthcare provider establishes a data infrastructure that includes electronic health records (EHRs), patient monitoring systems, and a data warehouse. This infrastructure collects and stores patient data, vital signs, and treatment histories.

Data Preparation

Data scientists clean and preprocess the data to ensure accuracy and consistency. This involves handling missing values, normalizing data formats, and creating relevant features such as patient demographics, medical history, and treatment responses.

Model Development

Several AI models are developed to address different aspects of healthcare:

- **Predictive Analytics**: Machine learning models predict patient outcomes based on historical data. These models identify patients at risk of complications and recommend preventive measures.
- **Natural Language Processing (NLP)**: NLP models process unstructured data from medical records, extracting valuable information such as symptoms, diagnoses, and treatment plans.
- **Computer Vision**: AI-powered computer vision systems analyze medical images, such as X-rays and MRIs, to detect anomalies and assist in diagnosis.

Integration and Testing

The AI models are integrated into the healthcare provider's systems. Predictive analytics models are used in patient monitoring systems to provide real-time alerts for high-risk patients. NLP models are integrated with EHRs to automate data extraction and documentation. Computer vision systems are deployed in radiology departments to assist with image analysis.

Extensive testing is conducted to ensure that the AI models perform accurately and reliably in clinical settings. This involves validating model predictions, verifying integration with existing systems, and ensuring compliance with healthcare regulations.

Deployment and Monitoring

The AI-enhanced healthcare systems are deployed to clinical environments. Monitoring tools track the performance of AI models, including prediction accuracy, alert rates, and user feedback. These tools also ensure that the AI systems operate within regulatory and ethical guidelines.

Continuous improvement processes are established to maintain and enhance the AI models. This includes regular retraining of models with new data, updating algorithms to incorporate the latest medical knowledge, and addressing user feedback to improve system usability.

Challenges and Solutions

Integrating AI into existing products comes with its set of challenges. Understanding these challenges and implementing effective solutions is crucial for successful AI integration.

1. **Data Privacy and Security**: Ensuring data privacy and security is paramount when integrating AI. Implement robust encryption, access controls, and compliance with regulations such as GDPR to protect user data.
2. **Scalability**: AI models need to scale efficiently to handle increasing volumes of data and user interactions. Use cloud-based solutions and distributed computing frameworks to ensure scalability.
3. **User Adoption**: Gaining user trust and encouraging adoption of AI-enhanced features can be challenging. Provide clear explanations of AI functionalities, offer user training, and gather feedback to improve user experience.
4. **Bias and Fairness**: AI models can inadvertently introduce bias into decision-making processes. Implement fairness metrics, conduct regular audits, and use diverse training data to mitigate bias.
5. **Maintenance and Updates**: AI models require regular maintenance and updates to remain effective. Establish a process for continuous monitoring, retraining, and updating models based on new data and changing requirements.

Integrating AI into existing products is a transformative journey that offers significant benefits in terms of enhanced functionality, improved user experience, and competitive advantage. By following a strategic approach, addressing technical requirements, and implementing practical steps, businesses can successfully incorporate AI into their products. The ongoing process of continuous improvement ensures that AI-enhanced products remain relevant, effective, and aligned with evolving user needs and market trends.

In the next sections of this chapter, we will explore how to design new AI-powered products, understand the ethical considerations in AI development, and examine the future trends in AI product innovation. Each section will provide in-depth insights and practical guidance for building AI-powered products that deliver exceptional value and drive business success.

Developing New AI-Centric Solutions

Creating new AI-centric solutions involves a comprehensive process that spans ideation, design, development, and deployment. This section explores the essential steps, best practices, and key considerations for developing innovative AI-powered products from scratch.

Ideation and Conceptualization

The journey of developing AI-centric solutions begins with ideation and conceptualization. This stage involves identifying opportunities where AI can add value and brainstorming potential applications.

Identifying Opportunities

1. **Market Research**: Conduct thorough market research to understand current trends, gaps, and opportunities. Identify industries or sectors where AI can address unmet needs or enhance existing processes.
2. **Customer Pain Points**: Engage with potential users to uncover their pain points and challenges. Understanding customer needs helps in identifying areas where AI can provide significant improvements.
3. **Competitive Analysis**: Analyze existing AI products and solutions in the market. Identify their strengths, weaknesses, and areas where your solution can offer a unique advantage.

Brainstorming and Idea Generation

1. **Cross-Functional Collaboration**: Involve cross-functional teams, including data scientists, engineers, designers, and domain experts, in brainstorming sessions. Diverse perspectives foster creativity and innovative thinking.
2. **Use Case Development**: Develop detailed use cases that describe how the AI solution will be used, the problems it will

solve, and the benefits it will provide. Use cases help in visualizing the practical applications and potential impact of the solution.

3.   **Feasibility Assessment**: Evaluate the feasibility of each idea based on factors such as technical complexity, data availability, resource requirements, and potential return on investment. Prioritize ideas that are feasible and offer substantial value.

Design and Planning

Once a viable idea is identified, the next step is to design and plan the AI solution. This stage involves defining the architecture, selecting the right technologies, and creating a detailed project plan.

Defining the Architecture

1.   **System Architecture**: Define the overall system architecture, including the components, their interactions, and the data flow. Ensure that the architecture is scalable, modular, and robust.
2.   **Data Architecture**: Design the data architecture to support the AI models. This includes data sources, storage solutions, data pipelines, and data preprocessing steps.
3.   **Model Architecture**: Select the appropriate AI models and define their architecture. Consider factors such as model complexity, performance, and the specific requirements of the use case.

Selecting Technologies

1.   **Programming Languages**: Choose the programming languages and frameworks that are best suited for AI development. Popular choices include Python, TensorFlow, PyTorch, and R.
2.   **Tools and Libraries**: Identify the tools and libraries needed for data preprocessing, model training, evaluation, and deployment. Ensure that the chosen tools are compatible with the overall system architecture.

3.   **Infrastructure**: Select the infrastructure for development and deployment. This may include cloud platforms, on-premises servers, or hybrid solutions. Ensure that the infrastructure supports scalability, security, and performance requirements.

Creating a Project Plan

1.   **Milestones and Timelines**: Define key milestones and create a detailed timeline for the project. Break down the development process into manageable phases, such as data collection, model development, integration, and testing.

2.   **Resource Allocation**: Allocate resources, including personnel, budget, and tools, to each phase of the project. Ensure that the team has the necessary skills and support to execute the project successfully.

3.   **Risk Management**: Identify potential risks and develop mitigation strategies. Common risks include data quality issues, technical challenges, and changing requirements. Regularly review and update the risk management plan.

Development and Testing

The development and testing phase is where the AI solution is brought to life. This stage involves data collection, model development, integration, and rigorous testing to ensure the solution meets its objectives.

Data Collection and Preparation

1.   **Data Sources**: Identify and secure the data sources needed for training the AI models. This may include structured data, unstructured data, real-time data, and historical data.

2.   **Data Quality**: Ensure the quality of the data by implementing data cleaning and preprocessing steps. Address issues such as missing values, outliers, and inconsistencies to improve the reliability of the AI models.

3. **Data Augmentation**: Use data augmentation techniques to enhance the training dataset. This may involve generating synthetic data, expanding the dataset with additional features, or combining data from multiple sources.

Model Development

1. **Algorithm Selection**: Choose the appropriate algorithms based on the specific requirements of the use case. Consider factors such as accuracy, interpretability, and computational efficiency.
2. **Model Training**: Train the AI models using the prepared data. This involves feeding the data into the algorithms, adjusting parameters, and optimizing the models to achieve the desired performance.
3. **Evaluation and Tuning**: Evaluate the performance of the models using validation and test datasets. Fine-tune the models by adjusting hyperparameters, experimenting with different architectures, and addressing any identified issues.

Integration and Testing

1. **System Integration**: Integrate the AI models with the existing systems and applications. Develop APIs, user interfaces, and backend systems to enable seamless interaction between the AI components and other product features.
2. **Testing**: Conduct thorough testing to ensure that the AI solution performs as expected. This includes functional testing, performance testing, and user acceptance testing. Identify and resolve any issues or bugs.
3. **Validation**: Validate the AI models in real-world scenarios to ensure they generalize well to new data. Collect feedback from users and stakeholders to assess the effectiveness and usability of the solution.

Deployment and Maintenance

The deployment and maintenance phase involves rolling out the AI solution to production environments and ensuring its ongoing performance and improvement.

Deployment

1. **Deployment Strategy**: Define a deployment strategy that outlines the steps for rolling out the AI solution. This may include phased deployment, A/B testing, or pilot programs to minimize risks and gather feedback.
2. **Infrastructure Setup**: Set up the necessary infrastructure to support the AI solution in production. Ensure that the infrastructure is scalable, secure, and capable of handling the expected load.
3. **Monitoring and Management**: Implement monitoring tools to track the performance of the AI solution in real-time. Monitor key metrics, detect anomalies, and gather user feedback to identify areas for improvement.

Maintenance and Continuous Improvement

1. **Model Retraining**: Regularly retrain the AI models with new data to ensure they remain accurate and relevant. Address any drift in model performance and update the models as needed.
2. **Performance Optimization**: Continuously optimize the performance of the AI solution by fine-tuning algorithms, improving data quality, and enhancing system architecture.
3. **User Feedback**: Collect and analyze feedback from users to identify pain points and areas for improvement. Use this feedback to guide future enhancements and ensure the solution meets user needs.
4. **Scalability and Expansion**: Plan for scalability and expansion of the AI solution. This may involve adding new features, supporting additional use cases, or expanding to new markets.

Ethical and Regulatory Considerations

Developing AI-centric solutions also requires attention to ethical and regulatory considerations. Ensuring fairness, transparency, and compliance with regulations is crucial for building trust and maintaining the integrity of the solution.

Ethical Considerations

1. **Bias and Fairness**: Implement measures to detect and mitigate bias in AI models. Use diverse training data, conduct fairness audits, and ensure that the models do not discriminate against any group.
2. **Transparency**: Ensure transparency in the development and deployment of AI solutions. Provide clear explanations of how the models work, the data they use, and the decisions they make.
3. **Privacy**: Protect user privacy by implementing robust data protection measures. Anonymize data, secure user consent, and comply with data privacy regulations.

Regulatory Compliance

1. **Industry Regulations**: Understand and comply with industry-specific regulations related to AI and data usage. This may include healthcare regulations, financial regulations, and consumer protection laws.
2. **Data Protection Laws**: Ensure compliance with data protection laws such as GDPR, CCPA, and HIPAA. Implement necessary safeguards to protect user data and ensure lawful data processing.
3. **Audit and Accountability**: Establish processes for auditing AI models and ensuring accountability. Regularly review and document model performance, decisions, and impacts.

Case Study: Developing an AI-Powered Personal Finance Assistant

To illustrate the process of developing a new AI-centric solution, let's consider the development of an AI-powered personal finance assistant. This solution aims to help users manage their finances, track expenses, and achieve their financial goals.

Ideation and Conceptualization

1. **Market Research**: Conduct market research to understand the growing demand for personal finance management tools and identify gaps in existing solutions.
2. **Customer Pain Points**: Engage with potential users to identify their pain points, such as difficulty tracking expenses, lack of financial planning, and challenges in achieving savings goals.
3. **Competitive Analysis**: Analyze existing personal finance apps to identify their strengths and weaknesses. Identify opportunities for differentiation, such as advanced budgeting features, personalized financial advice, and integration with banking services.

Design and Planning

1. **System Architecture**: Define the system architecture for the personal finance assistant. This includes components such as data aggregation, expense tracking, budgeting, and goal-setting modules.
2. **Data Architecture**: Design the data architecture to collect and process financial data from multiple sources, such as bank accounts, credit cards, and investment portfolios.
3. **Model Architecture**: Develop AI models for expense categorization, budget recommendations, and goal tracking. Choose appropriate algorithms for each use case, such as supervised learning for expense categorization and reinforcement learning for goal tracking.

Development and Testing

1.   **Data Collection and Preparation**: Collect financial data from users, ensuring data quality and consistency. Implement data cleaning and preprocessing steps to prepare the data for model training.
2.   **Model Development**: Develop and train AI models to categorize expenses, provide budget recommendations, and track progress towards financial goals. Evaluate model performance and fine-tune the models to achieve high accuracy.
3.   **Integration and Testing**: Integrate the AI models with the user interface and backend systems. Conduct thorough testing to ensure that the models perform accurately and the application provides a seamless user experience.

Deployment and Maintenance

1.   **Deployment Strategy**: Roll out the personal finance assistant to a pilot group of users to gather feedback and identify any issues. Gradually expand the user base as the solution is refined.
2.   **Monitoring and Management**: Implement monitoring tools to track the performance of the AI models and the overall application. Collect user feedback to identify areas for improvement and ensure the solution meets user needs.
3.   **Continuous Improvement**: Regularly retrain the AI models with new data to maintain accuracy and relevance. Continuously optimize the solution based on user feedback and performance metrics.

Ethical and Regulatory Considerations

1.   **Bias and Fairness**: Ensure that the AI models do not exhibit bias in expense categorization or budget recommendations. Conduct regular fairness audits and use diverse training data.

2. **Transparency**: Provide clear explanations of how the AI models work and how financial recommendations are generated. Ensure users understand and trust the system.

3. **Privacy**: Implement robust data protection measures to safeguard user financial data. Ensure compliance with data privacy regulations such as GDPR and CCPA.

Developing new AI-centric solutions is a multifaceted process that requires careful planning, technical expertise, and a focus on ethical and regulatory considerations. By following best practices in ideation, design, development, and deployment, businesses can create innovative AI-powered products that deliver exceptional value to users. Continuous improvement and adherence to ethical standards ensure that these solutions remain effective, trustworthy, and aligned with user needs.

In the subsequent sections of this chapter, we will delve into the ethical considerations in AI development and examine future trends in AI product innovation. Each section will provide valuable insights and practical guidance for building AI-powered products that drive business success and contribute to a more intelligent, efficient, and equitable future.

Challenges and Considerations

Developing and integrating AI-powered products come with a set of challenges and considerations that must be carefully addressed to ensure success. These challenges span technical, ethical, and organizational dimensions. This section explores the key challenges and provides strategies to navigate them effectively.

Technical Challenges

1. Data Quality and Availability

Challenge: High-quality, relevant data is the lifeblood of AI systems. However, obtaining clean, comprehensive, and labeled data can be challenging.

Considerations: Implement robust data governance practices, including data cleaning, normalization, and augmentation. Use data anonymization techniques to protect user privacy while gathering the necessary information.

2. Model Complexity and Performance

Challenge: Developing models that are both accurate and efficient can be complex, especially for tasks involving deep learning or natural language processing.

Considerations: Opt for models that balance complexity and performance. Employ techniques like hyperparameter tuning and model optimization to enhance performance. Continuously monitor model performance and make adjustments as needed.

3. Scalability

Challenge: Ensuring that AI solutions can scale to handle increasing volumes of data and users is critical but can be technically demanding.

Considerations: Use cloud-based infrastructures that offer scalability and flexibility. Implement distributed computing frameworks and load balancing to manage high volumes of data and traffic.

4.   **Integration with Legacy Systems**

Challenge: Integrating AI solutions with existing legacy systems can be cumbersome and may require significant modifications.

Considerations: Conduct thorough system assessments to identify integration points. Use APIs and middleware to facilitate seamless interaction between new AI components and legacy systems.

Ethical and Social Challenges

1.   **Bias and Fairness**

Challenge: AI systems can unintentionally perpetuate biases present in the training data, leading to unfair outcomes.

Considerations: Implement bias detection and mitigation techniques during model training. Ensure diverse and representative training datasets. Regularly audit AI systems for bias and take corrective actions.

2.   **Transparency and Explainability**

Challenge: Many AI models, especially deep learning models, are often seen as "black boxes" with decisions that are hard to interpret.

Considerations: Develop explainable AI models that provide insights into their decision-making processes. Use techniques such as LIME (Local Interpretable Model-agnostic Explanations) or SHAP (SHapley Additive exPlanations) to make AI decisions more transparent.

3.   Privacy and Data Security

Challenge: AI systems often require access to sensitive personal data, raising concerns about privacy and security.

Considerations: Implement strong encryption and access controls. Ensure compliance with data protection regulations such as GDPR and CCPA. Use differential privacy techniques to protect individual data while allowing aggregate analysis.

4.   Ethical Use of AI

Challenge: The ethical implications of AI deployment can affect public trust and acceptance.

Considerations: Develop and adhere to ethical guidelines for AI use. Engage stakeholders in discussions about the ethical implications of AI projects. Foster a culture of ethical responsibility within the organization.

Organizational Challenges

1.   Skill Gaps and Training

Challenge: Developing and maintaining AI solutions require specialized skills that may be lacking in the organization.

Considerations: Invest in training and upskilling programs for employees. Collaborate with academic institutions and industry partners to access the latest knowledge and expertise. Consider hiring specialized AI talent to fill critical roles.

2. Change Management

Challenge: Implementing AI solutions often requires changes in processes, workflows, and organizational culture.

Considerations: Develop a clear change management plan that includes communication strategies, training, and support for employees. Foster a culture of innovation and continuous improvement to facilitate AI adoption.

3. Cost and Resource Allocation

Challenge: AI projects can be resource-intensive, requiring significant investment in technology, data infrastructure, and talent.

Considerations: Conduct cost-benefit analyses to prioritize AI projects with the highest potential return on investment. Explore funding options, such as grants and partnerships, to support AI initiatives. Implement pilot projects to demonstrate value before scaling up.

4. Regulatory Compliance

Challenge: Ensuring compliance with regulatory requirements for AI and data usage can be complex and time-consuming.

Considerations: Stay informed about relevant regulations and industry standards. Develop compliance frameworks and engage legal experts to navigate regulatory challenges. Regularly audit AI systems to ensure ongoing compliance.

Summary

Building AI-powered products is a multifaceted endeavor that requires careful consideration of various challenges and factors. Integrating AI into existing products involves strategic planning, robust technical infrastructure, and continuous improvement. Developing new AI-centric solutions demands innovation, collaboration, and adherence to best practices in design, development, and deployment.

Throughout the process, it is crucial to address technical challenges such as data quality, model performance, scalability, and integration. Ethical and social challenges, including bias, transparency, privacy, and ethical use, must be carefully managed to build trust and ensure responsible AI deployment. Organizational challenges, such as skill gaps, change management, cost, and regulatory compliance, require strategic planning and resource allocation.

By navigating these challenges effectively, businesses can harness the transformative power of AI to create innovative products that deliver exceptional value. The journey of building AI-powered products is ongoing, with continuous improvement and adaptation needed to keep pace with technological advancements and evolving user needs.

Chapter 8: AI Agents in Decision Making

AI is reshaping the decision-making landscape across various domains. AI agents, with their advanced capabilities, are now integral to enhancing decision-making processes in business, healthcare, finance, and beyond. This chapter explores how AI agents contribute to decision-making, the technologies that drive them, practical applications, and the challenges and considerations involved.

The Role of AI Agents in Decision Making

AI agents assist in decision-making by analyzing vast amounts of data, identifying patterns, and providing actionable insights. They enable organizations to make informed, data-driven decisions that improve efficiency, reduce costs, and enhance outcomes. The key roles of AI agents in decision-making include:

1.   **Data Analysis and Interpretation**: AI agents can process and analyze large datasets quickly, extracting meaningful insights that inform decision-making.
2.   **Predictive Analytics**: By leveraging machine learning algorithms, AI agents predict future trends and outcomes, helping organizations anticipate changes and plan accordingly.
3.   **Optimization**: AI agents optimize decision-making by identifying the best possible solutions based on given constraints and objectives.
4.   **Automated Decision Making**: In certain scenarios, AI agents can make decisions autonomously, streamlining processes and reducing the need for human intervention.

Key Technologies Driving AI Decision Making

Several key technologies enable AI agents to enhance decision-making processes. These include machine learning, deep learning, natural language processing (NLP), and reinforcement learning.

1. Machine Learning

Machine learning is a core technology that enables AI agents to learn from data and improve their performance over time. It involves training algorithms on historical data to recognize patterns and make predictions.

Supervised Learning: Algorithms are trained on labeled data, learning to map inputs to outputs. This is useful for tasks like classification and regression.

Unsupervised Learning: Algorithms identify patterns in unlabeled data, useful for clustering and anomaly detection.

Semi-Supervised Learning: Combines labeled and unlabeled data to improve learning accuracy.

Reinforcement Learning: Algorithms learn by interacting with an environment, receiving feedback, and optimizing their actions to maximize rewards.

2. Deep Learning

Deep learning, a subset of machine learning, uses neural networks with multiple layers to model complex patterns in data. It is particularly effective for tasks like image recognition, natural language processing, and game playing.

Neural Networks: Composed of layers of interconnected nodes, neural networks can learn hierarchical representations of data.

Convolutional Neural Networks (CNNs): Specialized for processing grid-like data, such as images.

Recurrent Neural Networks (RNNs): Designed for sequential data, making them ideal for tasks like language modeling and time series prediction.

Transformer Models: Advanced architectures like BERT and GPT, which excel in natural language understanding and generation.

3.   **Natural Language Processing (NLP)**

NLP enables AI agents to understand, interpret, and generate human language, facilitating decision-making based on textual data.

Text Classification: Categorizes text into predefined classes, useful for spam detection and sentiment analysis.

Named Entity Recognition (NER): Identifies entities like names, dates, and locations within text.

Machine Translation: Translates text from one language to another.

Sentiment Analysis: Determines the sentiment expressed in text, useful for gauging public opinion and customer feedback.

4.   **Reinforcement Learning**

Reinforcement learning involves training AI agents to make decisions by rewarding desirable actions and penalizing undesirable ones. It is particularly useful for tasks that involve sequential decision-making and dynamic environments.

Policy Optimization: AI agents learn a policy that maps states to actions to maximize cumulative rewards.

Value-Based Methods: Agents learn to estimate the value of states or actions to make decisions.

Model-Based Methods: Agents build a model of the environment and use it to plan actions.

Practical Applications of AI in Decision Making

AI agents are applied across various sectors to enhance decision-making. Here are some practical applications:

1. Business and Operations

AI agents are used to optimize business operations, improve supply chain management, and enhance strategic planning.

Demand Forecasting: Machine learning models predict customer demand, helping businesses optimize inventory levels and reduce costs.

Supply Chain Optimization: AI agents analyze supply chain data to identify inefficiencies and recommend improvements.

Strategic Planning: AI-powered tools analyze market trends, competitor behavior, and internal performance data to inform strategic decisions.

Case Study: Walmart

Walmart uses AI agents to optimize its supply chain and inventory management. Machine learning models predict product demand, ensuring that stores are stocked with the right products at the right time. This reduces stockouts and overstock situations, improving customer satisfaction and reducing costs.

2. Healthcare

AI agents assist in medical decision-making, improving diagnostic accuracy, treatment planning, and patient outcomes.

Diagnostic Support: AI models analyze medical images, patient records, and lab results to assist doctors in diagnosing diseases.

Personalized Treatment: Machine learning algorithms analyze patient data to recommend personalized treatment plans.

Predictive Analytics: AI agents predict patient outcomes, helping healthcare providers identify high-risk patients and intervene early.

Case Study: IBM Watson Health

IBM Watson Health uses AI to support medical decision-making. The system analyzes vast amounts of medical literature, patient records, and clinical data to assist doctors in diagnosing diseases and recommending treatments. Watson's ability to process and interpret complex medical data enhances the accuracy and efficiency of healthcare delivery.

3.   **Finance**

In the finance sector, AI agents are used for risk management, investment strategies, and fraud detection.

Risk Management: AI models assess credit risk, market risk, and operational risk, helping financial institutions make informed decisions.

Investment Strategies: Machine learning algorithms analyze market data to identify investment opportunities and optimize portfolios.

Fraud Detection: AI agents analyze transaction data to detect and prevent fraudulent activities.

Case Study: JPMorgan Chase

JPMorgan Chase employs AI agents to enhance its risk management and investment strategies. Machine learning models analyze financial data to assess credit risk and detect fraudulent transactions. AI-driven investment platforms provide personalized investment advice and optimize portfolio management.

4. Marketing and Sales

AI agents improve marketing and sales by analyzing customer data, optimizing campaigns, and enhancing customer engagement.

Customer Segmentation: Machine learning algorithms segment customers based on their behavior and preferences, allowing for targeted marketing.

Campaign Optimization: AI models predict the effectiveness of marketing campaigns and suggest adjustments to maximize ROI.

Customer Engagement: AI-powered chatbots and virtual assistants engage with customers, providing personalized recommendations and support.

Case Study: Netflix

Netflix uses AI agents to optimize its marketing and content recommendation strategies. Machine learning algorithms analyze viewing patterns and preferences to suggest personalized content, improving customer engagement and retention. AI-driven marketing campaigns target users with relevant promotions, enhancing the effectiveness of marketing efforts.

5. Manufacturing

AI agents optimize manufacturing processes, improve quality control, and enhance predictive maintenance.

Process Optimization: Machine learning models analyze production data to identify inefficiencies and suggest improvements.

Quality Control: AI-powered vision systems inspect products for defects, ensuring high quality and consistency.

Predictive Maintenance: AI agents predict equipment failures and recommend maintenance schedules to prevent downtime.

Case Study: General Electric (GE)

General Electric uses AI agents to enhance its manufacturing processes. Predictive maintenance models analyze sensor data from equipment to predict failures and schedule maintenance, reducing downtime and costs. AI-powered quality control systems inspect products for defects, ensuring high quality and consistency.

Challenges and Considerations

While AI agents offer significant benefits in decision-making, several challenges and considerations must be addressed to ensure successful implementation.

1. **Data Quality and Availability**

Challenge: High-quality data is essential for training accurate AI models, but obtaining and maintaining such data can be challenging.

Considerations: Implement robust data governance practices, including data cleaning, validation, and augmentation. Ensure continuous data collection and updating to maintain model accuracy.

2. Model Interpretability

Challenge: Many AI models, especially deep learning models, are complex and difficult to interpret, which can hinder trust and acceptance.

Considerations: Develop interpretable models and use techniques like LIME and SHAP to provide insights into model decisions. Ensure transparency in how AI models are developed and deployed.

3. Bias and Fairness

Challenge: AI models can inadvertently introduce bias, leading to unfair or discriminatory outcomes.

Considerations: Use diverse and representative training data. Implement fairness metrics and conduct regular audits to detect and mitigate bias. Ensure that AI models comply with ethical guidelines and regulations.

4. Ethical and Legal Compliance

Challenge: Ensuring that AI decision-making processes adhere to ethical standards and legal regulations is critical.

Considerations: Develop and enforce ethical guidelines for AI use. Ensure compliance with relevant laws and regulations, such as GDPR and CCPA. Establish accountability mechanisms to oversee AI decision-making.

5. Scalability and Deployment

Challenge: Scaling AI solutions and integrating them into existing systems can be complex and resource-intensive.

Considerations: Use scalable infrastructure, such as cloud platforms, to support AI deployment. Develop modular AI solutions that can be easily integrated and scaled. Plan for ongoing maintenance and updates to ensure long-term success.

6. **Human-AI Collaboration**

Challenge: Balancing human and AI decision-making can be challenging, especially in scenarios that require human judgment and expertise.

Considerations: Foster collaboration between human experts and AI agents. Use AI to augment human decision-making, providing insights and recommendations while allowing humans to make the final decisions. Ensure that AI systems are designed to support and enhance human capabilities.

Future Trends in AI-Driven Decision Making

The future of AI-driven decision making holds exciting possibilities as technology continues to advance. Here are some trends to watch:

1. **Explainable AI (XAI)**

As the demand for transparency and accountability in AI decision-making grows, explainable AI will become increasingly important. XAI aims to make AI models more interpretable, providing clear explanations for their decisions and enhancing trust.

2. **Real-Time Decision Making**

Advances in computational power and data processing will enable AI agents to make decisions in real-time, enhancing their ability to respond to dynamic environments and rapidly changing conditions.

3. Edge AI

Edge AI involves deploying AI models on edge devices, such as smartphones and IoT devices, rather than relying on centralized cloud infrastructure. This approach reduces latency and enables real-time decision making at the edge of the network.

4. Ethical AI Frameworks

The development of comprehensive ethical AI frameworks will guide the responsible use of AI in decision-making. These frameworks will address issues such as bias, fairness, privacy, and accountability, ensuring that AI systems are used ethically and responsibly.

5. Collaborative AI

Collaborative AI involves AI agents working alongside humans, enhancing their decision-making capabilities and supporting human expertise. This approach emphasizes human-AI collaboration, leveraging the strengths of both to achieve better outcomes.

Summary

AI agents are transforming decision-making across various domains, offering enhanced data analysis, predictive analytics, optimization, and automation. Key technologies such as machine learning, deep learning, NLP, and reinforcement learning drive these capabilities. Practical applications in business, healthcare, finance, marketing, and manufacturing demonstrate the profound impact of AI on decision-making processes.

However, several challenges and considerations must be addressed to ensure the successful implementation of AI agents. These include data quality, model interpretability, bias and fairness, ethical and legal compliance, scalability, and human-AI collaboration. By navigating these challenges and leveraging emerging trends, organizations can harness the full potential of AI-driven decision-making to achieve superior outcomes and drive innovation.

Chapter 9: Operational Efficiency and Cost Reduction

AI and AI agents are at the forefront of transforming business operations by enhancing efficiency and reducing costs. From streamlining processes to automating repetitive tasks, AI offers numerous opportunities to improve operational efficiency across various industries. This chapter delves into how AI agents can drive operational efficiency and cost reduction, exploring key technologies, practical applications, and strategic considerations.

The Role of AI in Enhancing Operational Efficiency

AI agents enhance operational efficiency by automating processes, optimizing resource allocation, and providing actionable insights. These intelligent systems can handle tasks that are time-consuming, repetitive, or prone to human error, allowing businesses to focus on more strategic activities. The primary roles of AI in enhancing operational efficiency include:

1.   **Process Automation**: AI agents automate routine and repetitive tasks, reducing manual effort and minimizing errors.
2.   **Resource Optimization**: AI systems optimize the use of resources, including labor, materials, and energy, to improve efficiency and reduce waste.
3.   **Predictive Maintenance**: AI agents predict equipment failures and recommend maintenance schedules, reducing downtime and maintenance costs.
4.   **Supply Chain Optimization**: AI-driven analytics optimize supply chain operations, from inventory management to logistics and transportation.
5.   **Data-Driven Decision Making**: AI agents analyze large datasets to provide insights that inform decision-making and strategy.

Key Technologies Driving Operational Efficiency

Several key technologies enable AI agents to enhance operational efficiency. These technologies include machine learning, robotic process automation (RPA), computer vision, and natural language processing (NLP).

1. Machine Learning

Machine learning is a core technology that enables AI agents to learn from data and improve their performance over time. It plays a crucial role in various applications that enhance operational efficiency.

Predictive Analytics: Machine learning models analyze historical data to predict future trends and events, such as equipment failures, demand fluctuations, and market changes.

Optimization Algorithms: These algorithms identify the most efficient ways to allocate resources, schedule tasks, and manage operations.

Anomaly Detection: Machine learning algorithms detect anomalies in data, such as defects in manufacturing processes or irregularities in financial transactions.

2. Robotic Process Automation (RPA)

RPA uses software robots to automate repetitive tasks and processes. It is particularly useful for tasks that involve structured data and predefined rules.

Data Entry and Processing: RPA bots automate data entry, extraction, and processing tasks, reducing manual effort and errors.

Workflow Automation: RPA automates workflows across different systems and applications, streamlining processes and improving efficiency.

Customer Service: RPA bots handle routine customer service tasks, such as responding to inquiries, processing orders, and updating records.

3. **Computer Vision**

Computer vision enables AI systems to interpret and understand visual information from images and videos. It has numerous applications in enhancing operational efficiency.

Quality Control: Computer vision systems inspect products for defects and ensure quality standards are met in manufacturing processes.

Surveillance and Security: AI-powered surveillance systems monitor facilities, detect security breaches, and alert security personnel.

Inventory Management: Computer vision systems track inventory levels, detect discrepancies, and manage stock in real-time.

4. **Natural Language Processing (NLP)**

NLP enables AI agents to understand and interpret human language, facilitating communication and automating tasks that involve textual data.

Document Processing: NLP algorithms extract and process information from documents, such as invoices, contracts, and reports.

Customer Support: AI-powered chatbots use NLP to handle customer inquiries, provide support, and resolve issues.

Voice Assistants: NLP powers voice-activated assistants that automate tasks, provide information, and improve user experience.

Practical Applications of AI for Operational Efficiency

AI agents are applied across various industries to enhance operational efficiency. Here are some practical applications:

1. Manufacturing

AI agents optimize manufacturing processes, improve quality control, and enhance predictive maintenance.

Process Optimization: Machine learning models analyze production data to identify inefficiencies and suggest improvements, such as adjusting machine settings or reconfiguring workflows.

Quality Control: Computer vision systems inspect products for defects, ensuring high quality and consistency. AI algorithms also analyze production data to detect patterns that may indicate quality issues.

Predictive Maintenance: AI agents predict equipment failures and recommend maintenance schedules based on historical data and real-time sensor inputs. This proactive approach reduces downtime and maintenance costs.

Case Study: Siemens

Siemens uses AI to enhance its manufacturing operations. Predictive maintenance models analyze sensor data from equipment to predict failures and schedule maintenance, reducing downtime and costs. AI-powered quality control systems inspect products for defects, ensuring high quality and consistency.

2. Supply Chain and Logistics

AI agents optimize supply chain operations, from inventory management to logistics and transportation.

Inventory Management: AI algorithms predict demand, optimize inventory levels, and automate reordering processes. This reduces stockouts and overstock situations, improving efficiency and reducing costs.

Logistics Optimization: Machine learning models optimize transportation routes, schedules, and fleet management to minimize costs and improve delivery times.

Supplier Management: AI agents analyze supplier performance, identify risks, and recommend strategies for supplier selection and management.

Case Study: DHL

DHL uses AI to optimize its logistics operations. Machine learning models analyze transportation data to optimize routes and schedules, reducing fuel consumption and delivery times. AI-powered inventory management systems ensure that warehouses are stocked with the right products at the right time.

3. Retail

AI agents enhance operational efficiency in retail by optimizing inventory, improving customer service, and personalizing the shopping experience.

Demand Forecasting: Machine learning models predict customer demand, helping retailers optimize inventory levels and reduce stockouts.

Customer Service: AI-powered chatbots handle customer inquiries, process orders, and provide support, reducing the workload on human agents.

Personalization: AI algorithms analyze customer data to provide personalized recommendations, improving customer satisfaction and driving sales.

Case Study: Walmart

Walmart uses AI to optimize its retail operations. Machine learning models predict product demand, ensuring that stores are stocked with the right products at the right time. AI-powered chatbots handle customer inquiries and provide personalized recommendations, enhancing the customer experience.

4.   **Healthcare**

AI agents improve operational efficiency in healthcare by streamlining administrative tasks, enhancing patient care, and supporting medical decision-making.

Appointment Scheduling: AI-powered systems automate appointment scheduling, reminders, and cancellations, reducing administrative workload and improving patient satisfaction.

Medical Imaging: AI algorithms analyze medical images to assist radiologists in detecting anomalies and diagnosing diseases, improving accuracy and efficiency.

Patient Monitoring: AI agents monitor patient vital signs, predict health issues, and recommend interventions, reducing hospital readmissions and improving patient outcomes.

Case Study: Cleveland Clinic

Cleveland Clinic uses AI to enhance its healthcare operations. AI-powered systems automate appointment scheduling and reminders, reducing administrative workload and improving patient satisfaction. Machine learning algorithms analyze medical images to assist radiologists in detecting anomalies and diagnosing diseases, improving accuracy and efficiency.

5.   **Energy and Utilities**

AI agents optimize energy production, enhance grid management, and improve maintenance processes in the energy and utilities sector.

Energy Production Optimization: Machine learning models analyze consumption patterns and environmental data to optimize energy production and reduce costs.

Grid Management: AI algorithms monitor and manage the electrical grid, predicting demand, detecting faults, and optimizing energy distribution.

Predictive Maintenance: AI agents predict equipment failures in power plants and utility infrastructure, recommending maintenance schedules to reduce downtime and maintenance costs.

Case Study: General Electric (GE)

General Electric uses AI to optimize its energy operations. Machine learning models analyze consumption patterns and environmental data to optimize energy production and reduce costs. AI-powered grid management systems monitor and manage the electrical grid, predicting demand and detecting faults.

6. Finance and Banking

AI agents enhance operational efficiency in finance and banking by automating processes, improving risk management, and enhancing customer service.

Process Automation: RPA bots automate routine tasks such as data entry, transaction processing, and account management, reducing manual effort and errors.

Risk Management: Machine learning models analyze financial data to assess credit risk, detect fraud, and manage investment portfolios.

Customer Service: AI-powered chatbots handle customer inquiries, process transactions, and provide financial advice, reducing the workload on human agents.

Case Study: JPMorgan Chase

JPMorgan Chase employs AI to enhance its banking operations. RPA bots automate routine tasks such as data entry and transaction processing, reducing manual effort and errors. Machine learning models analyze financial data to assess credit risk and detect fraudulent transactions.

Strategic Considerations for Implementing AI

Implementing AI to enhance operational efficiency and reduce costs requires careful planning and strategic considerations. Here are some key factors to consider:

1. Aligning AI with Business Goals

Define Objectives: Clearly define the objectives of AI implementation, aligning them with overall business goals. Identify specific areas where AI can provide the most value, such as process automation, resource optimization, or predictive maintenance.

Measure Success: Establish metrics to measure the success of AI initiatives. These could include efficiency improvements, cost savings, error reduction, or customer satisfaction.

2.   **Data Management**

Data Quality: Ensure high-quality data for training AI models. Implement data governance practices, including data cleaning, validation, and augmentation.

Data Integration: Integrate data from various sources to provide a comprehensive view of operations. This may involve consolidating data from different systems, sensors, and databases.

3.   **Technology and Infrastructure**

Scalable Infrastructure: Invest in scalable infrastructure, such as cloud computing, to support AI implementation. Ensure that the infrastructure can handle large volumes of data and support real-time processing.

Integration with Existing Systems: Ensure seamless integration of AI solutions with existing systems and processes. Use APIs, middleware, and other integration tools to facilitate this.

4.   **Talent and Expertise**

Skill Development: Invest in training and upskilling employees to work with AI technologies. This may involve hiring new talent with specialized skills or providing training programs for existing staff.

Cross-Functional Teams: Form cross-functional teams that include data scientists, engineers, domain experts, and business leaders. This fosters collaboration and ensures that AI initiatives are aligned with business goals.

5. Ethical and Regulatory Considerations

Ethical AI Use: Develop and enforce ethical guidelines for AI use. Ensure that AI systems are designed and implemented in a way that respects privacy, fairness, and transparency.

Regulatory Compliance: Ensure compliance with relevant laws and regulations, such as GDPR and CCPA. Implement data protection measures and conduct regular audits to ensure ongoing compliance.

6. Change Management

Stakeholder Engagement: Engage stakeholders early in the AI implementation process. Communicate the benefits and objectives of AI initiatives, and address any concerns or resistance.

Training and Support: Provide training and support to employees to help them adapt to new AI-powered processes and systems. Offer resources and assistance to ensure a smooth transition.

Future Trends in AI for Operational Efficiency

The future of AI in enhancing operational efficiency and reducing costs holds exciting possibilities as technology continues to advance. Here are some trends to watch:

1. AI and IoT Integration

The integration of AI and the Internet of Things (IoT) will enable more efficient and intelligent operations. IoT devices will generate vast amounts of data that AI agents can analyze to optimize processes, predict maintenance needs, and enhance decision-making.

2. Edge AI

Edge AI involves deploying AI models on edge devices, such as sensors and IoT devices, rather than relying on centralized cloud infrastructure. This approach reduces latency and enables real-time decision-making at the edge of the network.

3. Autonomous Systems

Autonomous systems, powered by AI, will become more prevalent in various industries. These systems can operate independently, making decisions and performing tasks without human intervention. Examples include autonomous vehicles, drones, and robots.

4. AI-Driven Innovation

AI will drive innovation by enabling new business models, products, and services. Organizations will leverage AI to identify new opportunities, optimize operations, and create value in ways that were previously not possible.

5. Sustainability and Energy Efficiency

AI will play a crucial role in promoting sustainability and energy efficiency. AI agents will optimize energy consumption, reduce waste, and support renewable energy initiatives, contributing to a more sustainable future.

Summary

AI agents are transforming operational efficiency across various industries by automating processes, optimizing resource allocation, and providing actionable insights. Key technologies such as machine learning, RPA, computer vision, and NLP drive these capabilities. Practical applications in manufacturing, supply chain and logistics, retail, healthcare, energy, and finance demonstrate the profound impact of AI on operational efficiency and cost reduction.

Implementing AI for operational efficiency requires careful planning and strategic considerations, including aligning AI with business goals, ensuring data quality, investing in scalable infrastructure, and addressing ethical and regulatory considerations. Future trends such as AI and IoT integration, edge AI, autonomous systems, AI-driven innovation, and sustainability will further enhance the potential of AI in driving operational efficiency.

By leveraging the power of AI, organizations can achieve significant efficiency improvements, cost savings, and competitive advantages, paving the way for a more intelligent and efficient future.

Chapter 10: AI Agents in Everyday Life

AI agents have seamlessly integrated into our daily lives, transforming how we interact with technology, manage our time, and navigate the world. From smart home devices to personalized recommendations, AI agents are enhancing convenience, efficiency, and personalization in unprecedented ways. This chapter explores the myriad ways AI agents are influencing everyday life, the underlying technologies, practical applications, and the implications for individuals.

The Role of AI Agents in Everyday Life

AI agents play a crucial role in various aspects of our daily routines, providing assistance, automation, and insights that enhance our quality of life. The primary roles of AI agents in everyday life include:

1.   **Personal Assistants**: AI-powered personal assistants like Siri, Alexa, and Google Assistant help manage tasks, answer questions, and control smart devices.
2.   **Smart Home Devices**: AI agents automate and optimize home functions, from lighting and heating to security and entertainment.
3.   **Health and Wellness**: AI-driven health applications monitor fitness, provide personalized health advice, and manage chronic conditions.
4.   **Entertainment and Media**: AI algorithms personalize content recommendations, enhancing our media consumption experience.
5.   **Navigation and Travel**: AI-powered navigation systems provide real-time traffic updates, route optimization, and travel planning.

Key Technologies Driving AI in Everyday Life

Several key technologies enable AI agents to seamlessly integrate into our daily lives. These technologies include natural language processing (NLP), machine learning, computer vision, the Internet of Things (IoT), and augmented reality (AR).

1.   Natural Language Processing (NLP)

NLP allows AI agents to understand, interpret, and generate human language, making interactions with technology more natural and intuitive.

Voice Recognition: NLP enables AI agents to recognize and respond to voice commands, facilitating hands-free interaction.

Sentiment Analysis: NLP algorithms analyze text to detect emotions and sentiments, enabling personalized responses.

Language Translation: NLP powers real-time language translation, breaking down communication barriers.

2.   Machine Learning

Machine learning algorithms enable AI agents to learn from data and improve their performance over time, providing personalized and context-aware experiences.

Recommendation Systems: Machine learning models analyze user behavior and preferences to recommend products, content, and services.

Predictive Analytics: These algorithms predict user needs and preferences, proactively offering assistance and suggestions.

Behavior Analysis: Machine learning analyzes patterns in user behavior to provide customized experiences and anticipate needs.

3. Computer Vision

Computer vision enables AI agents to interpret and understand visual information from images and videos, enhancing their ability to interact with the physical world.

Facial Recognition: AI agents use computer vision to recognize faces, enabling secure access and personalized experiences.

Object Detection: Computer vision identifies and tracks objects, enhancing applications like security, navigation, and augmented reality.

Image Analysis: AI-powered image analysis provides insights and recommendations based on visual content, such as identifying plant species or diagnosing skin conditions.

4. Internet of Things (IoT)

The Internet of Things (IoT) connects everyday devices to the internet, allowing them to collect and exchange data. AI agents leverage IoT to automate and optimize various aspects of our lives.

Smart Home Integration: IoT devices like smart thermostats, lights, and security cameras are controlled and optimized by AI agents. These devices collect data on user behavior, preferences, and environmental conditions to provide personalized and efficient home management.

Wearable Devices: IoT-enabled wearables monitor health metrics, providing real-time feedback and personalized recommendations. Wearables like fitness trackers and smartwatches collect data on physical activity, sleep patterns, and vital signs, which AI agents analyze to offer health insights and advice.

Connected Vehicles: AI agents enhance vehicle safety and efficiency through IoT connectivity, providing real-time traffic updates, autonomous driving capabilities, and vehicle diagnostics. Connected vehicles communicate with each other and with traffic infrastructure to optimize routes and improve safety.

5.   **Augmented Reality (AR)**

Augmented reality (AR) enhances real-world environments with digital overlays, providing interactive and immersive experiences. AI agents leverage AR to offer real-time information, assistance, and entertainment.

Interactive Interfaces: AR interfaces enable users to interact with digital content overlaid on the physical world, enhancing tasks such as navigation, gaming, and shopping.

Real-Time Information: AI agents provide real-time information through AR, such as displaying directions, identifying objects, or offering contextual data about the surroundings.

Enhanced Learning and Training: AR combined with AI creates immersive educational experiences, offering interactive lessons, simulations, and real-time feedback for various learning and training applications.

Practical Applications of AI in Everyday Life

AI agents are applied in various aspects of daily life, enhancing convenience, efficiency, and personalization. Here are some practical applications:

1.   **Smart Home Automation**

AI agents transform homes into smart environments, automating tasks and optimizing functions to improve comfort and efficiency.

Lighting and Climate Control: AI-powered systems adjust lighting and temperature based on user preferences, occupancy, and environmental conditions. Smart thermostats learn user habits to optimize heating and cooling, reducing energy consumption.

Security and Surveillance: AI-driven security systems monitor for intrusions, recognize faces, and alert homeowners to potential threats. These systems can differentiate between family members, guests, and unknown individuals, enhancing security and providing peace of mind.

Appliance Management: Smart appliances, such as refrigerators and washing machines, use AI to optimize energy usage and provide maintenance alerts. For example, smart refrigerators can track food inventory, suggest recipes, and notify users when items are running low.

Case Study: Nest Thermostat

The Nest Thermostat uses AI to learn user preferences and adjust the temperature accordingly. It analyzes patterns to optimize energy usage, reducing costs and improving comfort. The system also provides remote control and monitoring through a mobile app, enhancing convenience.

2.   **Personal Assistants**

AI-powered personal assistants help manage tasks, answer questions, and control smart devices, making daily routines more efficient.

Task Management: Personal assistants schedule appointments, set reminders, and manage to-do lists. They can integrate with calendars and email to provide seamless task management.

Information Retrieval: AI agents provide answers to questions, search the internet, and retrieve information on demand. They can offer weather updates, news briefings, and directions.

Smart Device Control: Personal assistants control smart home devices, such as lights, locks, and thermostats, through voice commands or mobile apps. They can create routines that automate multiple actions, like turning off lights and locking doors at bedtime.

Case Study: Amazon Alexa

Amazon Alexa is an AI-powered personal assistant that helps users manage tasks, control smart devices, and access information. Alexa's capabilities include playing music, providing weather updates, setting reminders, and controlling smart home devices, enhancing convenience and efficiency.

3.   **Health and Wellness**

AI agents support health and wellness by monitoring fitness, providing personalized health advice, and managing chronic conditions.

Fitness Tracking: AI-powered fitness apps and wearable devices track physical activity, monitor health metrics, and provide personalized workout recommendations. They can set fitness goals, track progress, and offer motivation.

Health Monitoring: AI agents monitor vital signs, track medication adherence, and provide alerts for potential health issues. They can detect irregularities in heart rate, blood pressure, and other metrics, prompting timely medical attention.

Mental Health Support: AI-driven mental health apps offer support, track mood, and provide resources for managing stress and anxiety. They can offer mindfulness exercises, stress-relief techniques, and connect users with mental health professionals.

Case Study: Fitbit

Fitbit uses AI to analyze health and fitness data from wearable devices. The system provides personalized workout recommendations, tracks sleep patterns, and monitors heart rate, helping users achieve their health and wellness goals.

4.   Entertainment and Media

AI agents enhance entertainment and media consumption by providing personalized content recommendations and improving the overall user experience.

Content Recommendations: AI algorithms analyze user preferences to recommend movies, music, books, and other content. They can curate playlists, suggest new shows, and provide tailored viewing experiences.

Content Creation: AI-powered tools assist in creating music, videos, and art, enabling new forms of creative expression. They can generate music tracks, edit videos, and create visual art based on user inputs.

Interactive Experiences: AI agents enhance gaming and virtual reality experiences by providing intelligent, adaptive interactions. They can create dynamic game environments, personalize storylines, and offer real-time feedback.

Case Study: Netflix

Netflix uses AI to personalize content recommendations for its users. Machine learning algorithms analyze viewing history, preferences, and behaviors to suggest movies and TV shows, enhancing the user experience and increasing engagement.

5. Navigation and Travel

AI agents improve navigation and travel planning by providing real-time traffic updates, route optimization, and personalized travel recommendations.

Real-Time Traffic Updates: AI-powered navigation systems provide real-time traffic updates, helping users avoid congestion and delays. They analyze traffic patterns, accidents, and road conditions to offer the best routes.

Route Optimization: AI algorithms optimize routes based on factors such as traffic, weather, and road conditions, improving travel efficiency. They can provide alternative routes and suggest the fastest or most fuel-efficient paths.

Travel Planning: AI agents assist with travel planning, offering personalized recommendations for destinations, accommodations, and activities. They can book flights, hotels, and rental cars, and create itineraries based on user preferences.

Case Study: Google Maps

Google Maps uses AI to provide real-time traffic updates, route optimization, and travel recommendations. The system analyzes traffic patterns, road conditions, and user preferences to provide accurate and efficient navigation, enhancing the travel experience.

6. Education and Personal Development

AI agents support education and personal development by providing personalized learning experiences, interactive content, and real-time feedback.

Personalized Learning: AI-powered educational platforms adapt to individual learning styles, pace, and preferences, providing customized learning paths and resources.

Interactive Content: AI agents create interactive and engaging educational content, such as virtual labs, simulations, and gamified learning experiences.

Skill Development: AI-driven applications help individuals develop new skills and knowledge, offering courses, tutorials, and real-time feedback to enhance learning outcomes.

Case Study: Duolingo

Duolingo uses AI to provide personalized language learning experiences. The platform adapts to each user's learning pace and style, offering customized exercises and feedback. AI algorithms analyze user performance to suggest areas for improvement and keep learners engaged.

Implications for Individuals

The integration of AI agents into everyday life has significant implications for individuals, impacting privacy, security, and the way we interact with technology.

1. **Privacy**

AI agents often require access to personal data to provide personalized experiences, raising concerns about privacy.

Data Collection: AI systems collect data on user behavior, preferences, and interactions, which can be sensitive.

Data Security: Ensuring the security of personal data is crucial to prevent unauthorized access and misuse.

Transparency: AI providers must be transparent about data collection practices and how data is used, offering users control over their information.

2. Security

As AI agents become more integrated into daily life, ensuring their security is essential to prevent vulnerabilities and cyberattacks.

Device Security: Securing smart home devices, personal assistants, and wearables is crucial to prevent unauthorized access and control.

Network Security: Ensuring the security of networks that connect AI devices is essential to protect data and prevent breaches.

Regular Updates: AI systems must be regularly updated to address security vulnerabilities and enhance protection.

3. Human Interaction

The increasing reliance on AI agents can impact human interaction and the way we relate to technology.

Convenience vs. Dependency: While AI agents enhance convenience, there is a risk of becoming overly dependent on technology for everyday tasks.

Digital Divide: Access to AI-powered technology can create disparities, with some individuals benefiting more than others.

Human-AI Collaboration: Promoting collaboration between humans and AI agents can enhance the benefits of technology while maintaining human control and oversight.

Future Trends in AI for Everyday Life

The future of AI in everyday life holds exciting possibilities as technology continues to advance. Here are some trends to watch:

1. Enhanced Personalization

AI agents will become increasingly adept at providing personalized experiences, tailoring interactions based on individual preferences, behaviors, and needs. This will enhance convenience, efficiency, and user satisfaction.

2. Ubiquitous AI

AI will become ubiquitous, integrated into a wide range of devices and applications. From smart home systems to wearable technology, AI agents will be seamlessly embedded into our daily routines.

3. Improved Natural Language Understanding

Advances in NLP will enable AI agents to understand and interpret human language more accurately and contextually. This will enhance the effectiveness of personal assistants and other AI-driven interactions.

4. AI and Augmented Reality (AR)

The integration of AI and AR will create immersive and interactive experiences, enhancing entertainment, education, and daily tasks. AI agents will provide real-time information and assistance in augmented reality environments.

Immersive Shopping Experiences: AR combined with AI will transform online and in-store shopping. Users can virtually try on clothes, visualize furniture in their homes, and receive personalized product recommendations.

Interactive Education: AI-powered AR applications will create engaging learning experiences. Students can explore historical events, conduct virtual science experiments, and receive real-time feedback on their performance.

Enhanced Navigation: AR navigation systems will overlay directions and points of interest onto the real world, providing intuitive and interactive guidance for walking, driving, or cycling.

5.   **Ethical AI**

As AI becomes more pervasive, ethical considerations will play a crucial role in its development and deployment. Ensuring fairness, transparency, and accountability in AI systems will be essential to maintain trust and promote responsible use.

Summary

AI agents are transforming everyday life by enhancing convenience, efficiency, and personalization across various aspects of daily routines. Key technologies such as NLP, machine learning, computer vision, IoT, and AR drive these capabilities. Practical applications in smart home automation, personal assistants, health and wellness, entertainment and media, navigation and travel, and education and personal development demonstrate the profound impact of AI on daily life.

The integration of AI agents into everyday life has significant implications for individuals, including privacy, security, and human interaction. Addressing these considerations is crucial to maximizing the benefits of AI while mitigating potential risks.

Future trends in AI for everyday life, such as enhanced personalization, ubiquitous AI, improved natural language understanding, AI and AR integration, and ethical AI, will further enhance the potential of AI agents to enrich our daily experiences and improve our quality of life. By embracing these advancements, individuals can navigate the evolving technological landscape and harness the full potential of AI in their everyday lives.

This revised structure ensures that Chapter 10 and Chapter 11 are distinct, with Chapter 10 focusing on the general integration of AI in daily life and Chapter 11 concentrating specifically on how AI enhances personal productivity.

Chapter 11: Enhancing Personal Productivity with AI Agents

In an era where efficiency and productivity are paramount, AI agents are emerging as invaluable tools for individuals striving to optimize their personal and professional lives. By automating routine tasks, managing schedules, and providing actionable insights, AI agents help individuals work smarter and achieve their goals more effectively. This chapter explores the various ways AI agents enhance personal productivity, supported by practical applications and future trends.

Task Management and Automation

One of the most significant ways AI agents enhance productivity is through task management and automation. By handling routine tasks, setting reminders, and organizing to-do lists, AI agents free up time for more important activities.

Automated Task Scheduling: AI agents analyze calendars and schedules to find optimal times for meetings, appointments, and tasks. They can automatically reschedule conflicts and adjust priorities based on changing circumstances.

Reminder Systems: AI agents set and manage reminders for tasks, deadlines, and appointments, ensuring nothing is forgotten. They can send notifications through multiple channels, such as email, text, and voice.

To-Do List Management: AI-powered to-do list apps categorize tasks, set priorities, and track progress. They can provide suggestions for task completion and remind users of pending tasks.

Case Study: Microsoft To-Do

Microsoft To-Do uses AI to enhance task management. The app integrates with Outlook and other Microsoft 365 tools to provide a unified view of tasks and deadlines. AI-powered suggestions help users prioritize tasks and manage their time effectively.

Time Management and Scheduling

Effective time management is crucial for productivity, and AI agents excel in optimizing schedules, identifying inefficiencies, and providing recommendations for better time allocation.

Calendar Integration: AI agents integrate with calendars to schedule meetings, set reminders, and optimize daily routines. They can suggest the best times for meetings based on participants' availability and preferences.

Time Blocking: AI agents help users allocate specific blocks of time for tasks, meetings, and breaks, improving focus and productivity. They can adjust time blocks based on task complexity and urgency.

Meeting Optimization: AI agents analyze meeting data to suggest improvements, such as reducing meeting duration, consolidating topics, and minimizing distractions.

Case Study: Google Calendar

Google Calendar uses AI to enhance time management and scheduling. The system suggests optimal meeting times based on participants' availability and preferences. AI-powered features like Smart Scheduling and Find a Time help users manage their schedules efficiently.

Information Retrieval and Organization

Efficient information retrieval and organization are critical for productivity. AI agents facilitate quick access to data, summarize content, and provide insights.

Document Search: AI-powered search engines quickly locate relevant documents and files based on keywords and context. They can search across multiple platforms and repositories, providing a unified view of information.

Content Summarization: AI agents summarize long documents, emails, and articles, highlighting key points and actionable items. This saves time and helps users quickly grasp important information.

Data Organization: AI-powered systems organize data into categories, tags, and folders, making it easy to find and manage. They can automatically classify emails, documents, and media based on content and context.

Case Study: Evernote

Evernote uses AI to enhance information retrieval and organization. The app's AI-powered search engine quickly locates notes and documents based on keywords and context. AI-driven features like note tagging and content categorization help users manage their information efficiently.

Email Management

Managing emails efficiently is a significant productivity booster. AI agents improve email management by automating tasks, prioritizing messages, and reducing inbox clutter.

Spam Filtering: AI algorithms identify and filter out spam and unwanted emails, reducing inbox clutter and distractions. They continuously learn from user behavior to improve filtering accuracy.

Email Categorization: AI-powered email clients categorize messages based on content and sender, prioritizing important emails and flagging less urgent ones. They can create folders and labels to organize emails automatically.

Automated Responses: AI agents generate suggested responses for common email inquiries, saving time and effort. They can also schedule follow-up emails and reminders.

Case Study: Gmail

Gmail uses AI to enhance email management. Features like Smart Reply and Smart Compose provide suggested responses and writing assistance. AI-powered spam filters and email categorization help users manage their inboxes efficiently.

Personal Analytics and Insights

AI agents provide personal analytics and insights, helping users understand their behavior, identify trends, and improve productivity.

Productivity Tracking: AI-powered productivity apps track work patterns, focus time, and task completion rates. They provide insights into how time is spent and suggest improvements for better time management.

Goal Setting and Tracking: AI agents help users set and track personal and professional goals, providing feedback and motivation. They can suggest milestones and actions to achieve goals effectively.

Behavior Analysis: AI algorithms analyze user behavior to identify habits and patterns that impact productivity. They provide personalized recommendations for optimizing workflows and improving efficiency.

Case Study: RescueTime

RescueTime uses AI to track and analyze user productivity. The app monitors time spent on various activities, providing insights into work patterns and distractions. AI-driven reports and recommendations help users improve focus and productivity.

Collaboration and Communication

AI agents enhance collaboration and communication by facilitating virtual meetings, managing project tasks, and providing real-time translation.

Virtual Meeting Assistance: AI-powered virtual meeting tools schedule, organize, and facilitate online meetings. They can transcribe meetings, highlight key points, and generate action items.

Project Management: AI agents manage project tasks, track progress, and allocate resources. They provide real-time updates and notifications to keep team members aligned and informed.

Real-Time Translation: AI-powered translation tools enable seamless communication across different languages, facilitating collaboration in global teams.

Case Study: Slack

Slack uses AI to enhance collaboration and communication. AI-powered features like message prioritization, smart notifications, and automated reminders help teams stay organized and productive. Integrations with project management tools provide real-time updates and task tracking.

Learning and Development

AI agents support learning and development by providing personalized learning experiences, interactive content, and real-time feedback.

Personalized Learning: AI-powered educational platforms adapt to individual learning styles, pace, and preferences, providing customized learning paths and resources.

Interactive Content: AI agents create interactive and engaging educational content, such as virtual labs, simulations, and gamified learning experiences.

Skill Development: AI-driven applications help individuals develop new skills and knowledge, offering courses, tutorials, and real-time feedback to enhance learning outcomes.

Case Study: Duolingo

Duolingo uses AI to provide personalized language learning experiences. The platform adapts to each user's learning pace and style, offering customized exercises and feedback. AI algorithms analyze user performance to suggest areas for improvement and keep learners engaged.

Future Trends in AI for Personal Productivity

The future of AI in enhancing personal productivity holds exciting possibilities as technology continues to advance. Here are some trends to watch:

1.   **Enhanced Personalization**

AI agents will become increasingly adept at providing personalized experiences, tailoring interactions based on individual preferences, behaviors, and needs. This will enhance convenience, efficiency, and user satisfaction.

2. Context-Aware Assistance

Future AI agents will be more context-aware, understanding the specific needs and preferences of users in real-time. This will enable them to provide more relevant and timely assistance, improving productivity.

3. Integrated Ecosystems

AI agents will be integrated into a wide range of devices and applications, creating a seamless and interconnected ecosystem. This will enable users to manage tasks, access information, and collaborate more efficiently.

4. Advanced Automation

Advances in AI and automation will enable AI agents to handle more complex tasks and processes, reducing the need for human intervention. This will free up time for higher-value activities and enhance overall productivity.

5. Ethical and Transparent AI

As AI becomes more pervasive, ethical considerations will play a crucial role in its development and deployment. Ensuring fairness, transparency, and accountability in AI systems will be essential to maintain trust and promote responsible use.

Summary

AI agents are transforming personal productivity by automating tasks, managing time effectively, and providing intelligent insights. Key technologies such as NLP, machine learning, computer vision, and RPA drive these capabilities. Practical applications in task management, time management, information retrieval, email management, personal analytics, collaboration, and learning demonstrate the profound impact of AI on personal productivity.

The integration of AI agents into personal productivity tools has significant implications, including enhanced efficiency, better time management, and improved decision-making. Addressing considerations such as privacy, security, and human interaction is crucial to maximizing the benefits of AI while mitigating potential risks.

Future trends in AI for personal productivity, such as enhanced personalization, context-aware assistance, integrated ecosystems, advanced automation, and ethical AI, will further enhance the potential of AI agents to improve our daily work and personal lives. By embracing these advancements, individuals can navigate the evolving technological landscape and harness the full potential of AI to boost their productivity and achieve their goals.

Chapter 12: AI Agents and Privacy

AI agents are increasingly embedded in our daily lives, offering unparalleled convenience, efficiency, and personalization. However, their widespread use raises significant privacy and ethical concerns. This chapter explores the ethical considerations, data security measures, and the delicate balance between convenience and privacy when using AI agents.

Ethical Considerations

The integration of AI agents into various aspects of life necessitates a thorough examination of the ethical implications. These considerations are crucial to ensure that AI systems are developed and deployed responsibly, safeguarding user rights and societal values.

1. Transparency and Explainability

Transparency: AI systems must be transparent in their operations, allowing users to understand how decisions are made. Transparency helps build trust and ensures accountability in AI systems.

Explainability: AI agents should be able to explain their actions and decisions in a way that is understandable to users. This is especially important in critical areas like healthcare, finance, and law enforcement, where decisions can have significant consequences.

2. Fairness and Bias

Fairness: AI systems must be designed to treat all users fairly, without discrimination based on race, gender, age, or other personal characteristics. Ensuring fairness involves using diverse and representative datasets to train AI models.

Bias: AI agents can inadvertently perpetuate or amplify biases present in the data they are trained on. It is essential to identify, measure, and mitigate biases in AI systems to prevent unfair treatment and discrimination.

3. Privacy and Consent

Privacy: Protecting user privacy is paramount in the design and deployment of AI systems. AI agents often require access to personal data to function effectively, but this must be balanced with robust privacy protections.

Consent: Users must be informed about the data being collected, how it will be used, and who it will be shared with. Obtaining informed consent is critical to respecting user autonomy and privacy.

4. Accountability and Responsibility

Accountability: There must be clear accountability for the actions and decisions made by AI systems. This involves assigning responsibility to developers, operators, and organizations that deploy AI agents.

Responsibility: Developers and organizations must take responsibility for the ethical implications of their AI systems. This includes conducting regular audits, addressing ethical concerns, and implementing corrective measures when necessary.

5. Autonomy and Human Agency

Autonomy: AI systems should support and enhance human autonomy rather than undermine it. Users should have control over how AI agents operate and make decisions on their behalf.

Human Agency: It is essential to ensure that AI agents do not replace human judgment in areas where human decision-making is critical. AI should augment human capabilities and assist in decision-making processes.

6. Security and Safety

Security: Ensuring the security of AI systems is crucial to protect them from malicious attacks and unauthorized access. Robust security measures must be in place to safeguard AI agents and the data they process.

Safety: AI agents must be designed and tested to operate safely, minimizing the risk of harm to users and society. This includes preventing unintended consequences and ensuring that AI systems behave as intended.

7. Impact on Employment and Society

Employment: The deployment of AI agents can lead to job displacement and changes in the workforce. It is essential to consider the social impact of AI on employment and implement measures to support affected workers.

Societal Impact: AI systems can have broad societal implications, influencing social norms, behaviors, and power dynamics. Ethical considerations must take into account the wider impact of AI on society and work towards inclusive and equitable outcomes.

Data Security

Data security is a critical aspect of using AI agents, as these systems often handle sensitive and personal information. Ensuring data security involves implementing robust measures to protect data from unauthorized access, breaches, and misuse.

1. Data Encryption

Encryption at Rest: Encrypting data stored on devices and servers helps protect it from unauthorized access. This includes encrypting databases, files, and backups.

Encryption in Transit: Encrypting data as it is transmitted over networks ensures that it remains secure during transfer. This includes using secure communication protocols such as HTTPS and TLS.

2.   **Access Controls**

Authentication: Implementing strong authentication mechanisms, such as multi-factor authentication (MFA), helps verify the identity of users accessing AI systems.

Authorization: Ensuring that users have appropriate access rights based on their roles and responsibilities helps prevent unauthorized access to sensitive data.

Audit Logs: Maintaining audit logs of access and actions performed on AI systems helps detect and investigate unauthorized activities.

3.   **Data Anonymization and Pseudonymization**

Anonymization: Removing personally identifiable information (PII) from datasets helps protect user privacy while allowing data to be used for analysis and AI training.

Pseudonymization: Replacing PII with pseudonyms reduces the risk of re-identification and enhances data privacy. Pseudonymized data can still be linked to individuals under controlled conditions.

4.   **Secure Data Storage**

Cloud Security: Using secure cloud storage solutions with robust security measures, such as encryption, access controls, and regular security assessments, helps protect data stored in the cloud.

On-Premises Security: Ensuring physical and digital security measures for data stored on-premises helps protect against unauthorized access and breaches.

5. Data Minimization and Retention

Data Minimization: Collecting only the minimum amount of data necessary for AI agents to function helps reduce the risk of data breaches and misuse.

Data Retention: Implementing data retention policies to securely delete data after it is no longer needed helps minimize the risk of unauthorized access and compliance with data protection regulations.

6. Regular Security Audits and Assessments

Vulnerability Assessments: Conducting regular vulnerability assessments helps identify and address security weaknesses in AI systems and their infrastructure.

Penetration Testing: Performing penetration testing simulates cyberattacks to evaluate the security of AI systems and identify potential vulnerabilities.

Security Audits: Regular security audits help ensure that security policies and practices are being followed and that AI systems remain secure over time.

7. Incident Response and Recovery

Incident Response Plan: Developing and maintaining an incident response plan helps organizations respond quickly and effectively to security incidents and breaches.

Data Recovery: Implementing data recovery measures, such as regular backups and disaster recovery plans, helps ensure data availability and integrity in case of security incidents.

8.   **Compliance with Data Protection Regulations**

Regulatory Compliance: Ensuring compliance with data protection regulations, such as the General Data Protection Regulation (GDPR) and the California Consumer Privacy Act (CCPA), helps protect user data and avoid legal consequences.

Privacy Impact Assessments (PIAs): Conducting PIAs helps organizations assess the privacy risks associated with AI systems and implement measures to mitigate those risks.

Balancing Convenience and Privacy

The integration of AI agents into everyday life offers significant convenience but also raises privacy concerns. Balancing these two aspects is essential to ensure that users can enjoy the benefits of AI while maintaining control over their personal data.

1.   **User Control and Consent**

Informed Consent: Providing clear and comprehensive information about data collection, usage, and sharing practices helps users make informed decisions and provide explicit consent.

User Control: Offering users control over their data, such as the ability to access, modify, or delete their information, helps maintain privacy and trust in AI systems.

Privacy Settings: Providing customizable privacy settings allows users to adjust the level of data sharing and personalization according to their preferences.

Expanded Details:

Granular Control: Allowing users to set permissions for different types of data and activities. For example, users might choose to share location data for navigation but not for targeted advertising.

Revocable Consent: Ensuring users can easily revoke their consent at any time, with their data promptly deleted or anonymized upon request.

Transparency Tools: Providing tools that show users how their data is being used and by whom, enhancing trust through transparency.

2.   **Data Transparency and Accountability**

Transparency Reports: Publishing transparency reports detailing data collection practices, usage, and sharing helps build trust and accountability.

Accountability Mechanisms: Implementing accountability mechanisms, such as regular audits and independent oversight, helps ensure that AI systems adhere to privacy and ethical standards.

Expanded Details:

Detailed Reporting: Transparency reports should include specifics on the types and amounts of data collected, the purposes for data use, and third parties involved in data processing.

Independent Audits: Conducting regular third-party audits to assess compliance with privacy policies and identify potential areas for improvement.

User-Friendly Summaries: Providing summaries of transparency reports in an accessible format, ensuring all users, regardless of technical expertise, can understand the privacy practices.

3. Privacy by Design

Design Principles: Incorporating privacy by design principles into the development of AI systems helps ensure that privacy is considered from the outset and throughout the system's lifecycle.

Privacy Enhancing Technologies (PETs): Using PETs, such as differential privacy and homomorphic encryption, helps protect user data while enabling AI agents to function effectively.

Expanded Details:

Lifecycle Privacy: Ensuring that privacy considerations are integrated at every stage of the AI system's development, from initial design to deployment and maintenance.

PET Implementation: Leveraging advanced privacy technologies like homomorphic encryption, which allows data to be processed in an encrypted form, thus never exposing the raw data.

User-Centric Design: Designing AI systems with user privacy preferences as a central feature, making privacy settings intuitive and easy to manage.

4. Ethical AI Development

Ethical Guidelines: Developing and following ethical guidelines for AI development helps ensure that AI systems respect user privacy and autonomy.

Stakeholder Involvement: Involving stakeholders, including users, ethicists, and regulators, in the development and deployment of AI systems helps address privacy and ethical concerns comprehensively.

Expanded Details:

Comprehensive Frameworks: Creating detailed ethical frameworks that cover various aspects of AI use, including data privacy, fairness, and transparency.

Stakeholder Workshops: Regularly holding workshops with diverse stakeholder groups to gather input on privacy practices and ethical concerns.

Ethical Impact Assessments: Conducting assessments to evaluate the potential ethical impacts of AI systems before deployment.

5.   **Balancing Personalization and Privacy**

Personalization Benefits: AI agents offer personalized experiences that enhance convenience and satisfaction. However, personalization often requires access to personal data.

Privacy Trade-Offs: Balancing the benefits of personalization with the need for privacy involves making informed decisions about data sharing and usage. Users should be aware of the trade-offs and have the ability to opt-out of certain data practices if desired.

Expanded Details:

Contextual Personalization: Providing personalization that respects privacy by using context-aware algorithms that only utilize data relevant to the immediate interaction.

User Education: Educating users on the benefits and risks of personalization, helping them make informed choices about their data.

Opt-Out Mechanisms: Offering clear and straightforward opt-out mechanisms for users who prefer not to have their data used for personalization.

6. **Building Trust**

Trustworthiness: Building trustworthy AI systems involves transparency, accountability, and ethical practices. Trustworthy AI agents are more likely to be accepted and valued by users.

User Education: Educating users about AI systems, their benefits, and their privacy implications helps build trust and empowers users to make informed decisions.

Expanded Details:

Consistent Communication: Maintaining open lines of communication with users regarding privacy practices and any changes to them.

Trust Signals: Implementing trust signals, such as certifications and compliance badges, that indicate adherence to privacy and ethical standards.

Feedback Mechanisms: Providing users with channels to give feedback on privacy concerns and suggestions for improvement.

7. **Future Directions**

Innovative Privacy Solutions: Exploring innovative privacy solutions, such as federated learning and privacy-preserving AI, can help balance convenience and privacy in AI systems.

Policy and Regulation: Developing policies and regulations that protect privacy while enabling innovation in AI can help address the challenges of balancing convenience and privacy.

Expanded Details:

Federated Learning: Utilizing federated learning to train AI models across decentralized devices using local data, ensuring that personal data remains on the user's device.

Adaptive Privacy Regulations: Advocating for adaptive regulations that evolve with technological advancements, providing robust privacy protections without stifling innovation.

Cross-Border Data Flow: Addressing the complexities of cross-border data flow with standardized international privacy frameworks.

Summary

AI agents offer significant benefits in terms of convenience, efficiency, and personalization, but they also raise important ethical and privacy concerns. Addressing these concerns involves considering transparency, fairness, privacy, consent, accountability, autonomy, security, and societal impact.

Data security is a critical aspect of using AI agents, requiring robust measures to protect data from unauthorized access, breaches, and misuse. Ensuring data security involves encryption, access controls, data anonymization, secure storage, data minimization, regular audits, incident response, and compliance with data protection regulations.

Balancing convenience and privacy is essential to ensure that users can enjoy the benefits of AI while maintaining control over their personal data. This involves providing user control, ensuring data transparency, incorporating privacy by design, following ethical guidelines, balancing personalization and privacy, building trust, and exploring innovative privacy solutions.

By addressing ethical considerations, ensuring data security, and balancing convenience and privacy, organizations can develop and deploy AI agents that respect user rights, enhance trust, and provide valuable benefits. The future of AI depends on the responsible and ethical use of these powerful technologies, ensuring that they serve the best interests of individuals and society.

Chapter 13: Implementing AI Agents in Your Business

AI agents are revolutionizing the way businesses operate, providing new opportunities for efficiency, innovation, and competitive advantage. Implementing AI agents in your business requires a strategic approach, encompassing understanding the technology, aligning it with business objectives, and addressing practical considerations. This chapter provides a comprehensive guide to implementing AI agents in your business, covering key steps, best practices, and potential challenges.

Aligning AI Agents with Business Objectives

Successful implementation of AI agents requires alignment with your business objectives and strategic goals. This alignment ensures that AI initiatives deliver tangible value and contribute to overall business success.

1. Identify Business Needs

Pain Points: Begin by identifying the key pain points and challenges within your organization that AI agents can address. Conduct interviews, surveys, and workshops with stakeholders to gather insights into areas where AI can add value.

Opportunities: Look for opportunities where AI can enhance existing processes, introduce new capabilities, or create competitive advantages. This might include improving customer service, optimizing supply chain operations, or enabling data-driven marketing strategies.

Use Cases: Develop specific use cases for AI agents that align with your business objectives. Prioritize use cases based on their potential impact, feasibility, and alignment with strategic goals.

Expanded Details:

Customer Service Improvement: If your organization faces challenges in providing timely and efficient customer service, AI agents can be deployed as chatbots or virtual assistants to handle routine inquiries, freeing up human agents to focus on more complex issues.

Operational Efficiency: Identify repetitive, time-consuming tasks that can be automated with AI agents, such as data entry, invoice processing, or inventory management, to improve operational efficiency and reduce costs.

Product Innovation: Explore how AI can be used to develop new products or services, such as personalized recommendations, predictive maintenance solutions, or AI-driven analytics tools.

2.   **Set Clear Goals**

Objectives: Define clear and measurable objectives for what you want to achieve with AI agents. Objectives should be specific, achievable, relevant, and time-bound (SMART). Examples include reducing customer response times by 50%, increasing sales conversion rates by 20%, or decreasing operational costs by 15%.

Metrics: Establish key performance indicators (KPIs) to measure the success of AI implementation. Common KPIs include customer satisfaction scores, response times, conversion rates, and cost savings. Metrics should align with your business objectives and provide actionable insights into the performance of AI agents.

Timeline: Develop a realistic timeline for implementation, including milestones and deadlines for each phase of the project. The timeline should account for planning, development, testing, deployment, and ongoing monitoring.

Expanded Details:

Customer Experience Metrics: Use metrics such as Net Promoter Score (NPS), Customer Effort Score (CES), and first contact resolution rate to measure the impact of AI agents on customer experience.

Operational Metrics: Track metrics such as processing time, error rates, and resource utilization to evaluate the efficiency gains achieved through AI automation.

Revenue Metrics: Monitor metrics like average order value, customer lifetime value, and revenue growth to assess the financial impact of AI-driven personalization and marketing efforts.

3. **Build a Business Case**

ROI Analysis: Conduct a comprehensive return on investment (ROI) analysis to justify the investment in AI agents. Consider both the costs (e.g., development, integration, training, and maintenance) and the potential benefits (e.g., cost savings, revenue growth, and improved customer satisfaction). Use scenario analysis to assess different implementation scenarios and their financial impact.

Stakeholder Buy-In: Engage key stakeholders early in the process to gain their support and buy-in for the AI project. This includes executives, managers, employees, and other relevant parties. Present a compelling business case that highlights the strategic importance, expected benefits, and risk mitigation strategies.

Resource Allocation: Identify the resources needed for implementation, including budget, personnel, and technology infrastructure. Ensure that you have the necessary expertise in AI, data science, and IT, either in-house or through external partnerships.

Expanded Details:

Cost-Benefit Analysis: Perform a detailed cost-benefit analysis that includes direct costs (e.g., software licenses, hardware, and development) and indirect costs (e.g., training and change management). Compare these costs against the anticipated benefits, such as cost savings, increased revenue, and improved operational efficiency.

Risk Assessment: Conduct a risk assessment to identify potential risks and challenges associated with AI implementation. Develop mitigation strategies to address these risks, such as contingency plans, phased rollouts, and ongoing monitoring.

Executive Support: Secure executive support by aligning the AI project with strategic business goals and demonstrating how it contributes to the overall vision and mission of the organization.

Steps to Implement AI Agents

Implementing AI agents involves several key steps, from planning and development to deployment and monitoring.

1. **Planning and Preparation**

Technology Assessment: Assess your existing technology infrastructure to determine if it can support AI agents. This includes evaluating hardware, software, and network capabilities.

Data Strategy: Develop a data strategy that outlines how data will be collected, stored, and used for AI. Ensure that you have access to high-quality, relevant data for training AI models.

Vendor Selection: If you decide to use third-party AI solutions, carefully evaluate vendors based on their capabilities, reputation, and alignment with your business needs.

2. **Development and Training**

AI Model Selection: Choose the appropriate AI models and algorithms for your use cases. Consider factors such as accuracy, scalability, and ease of integration.

Data Preparation: Collect and preprocess the data needed for training AI models. This includes cleaning, normalizing, and labeling data to ensure it is suitable for training.

Model Training: Train AI models using your prepared data. This involves feeding the data into the models, tuning hyperparameters, and iterating to improve performance.

Validation and Testing: Validate the AI models by testing them on separate datasets to ensure they generalize well to new data. Perform rigorous testing to identify and address any issues.

3.   **Integration and Deployment**

System Integration: Integrate AI agents with your existing systems and workflows. This may involve using APIs, middleware, or custom integration solutions.

User Training: Train employees and users on how to interact with and utilize AI agents effectively. Provide training materials, workshops, and support to ensure a smooth transition.

Pilot Deployment: Start with a pilot deployment to test AI agents in a real-world environment. Monitor performance, gather feedback, and make necessary adjustments before full-scale deployment.

4.   **Monitoring and Maintenance**

Performance Monitoring: Continuously monitor the performance of AI agents using your established KPIs. Track metrics such as accuracy, response times, user satisfaction, and cost savings.

Regular Updates: Regularly update AI models and algorithms to maintain their effectiveness. This includes retraining models with new data and incorporating feedback from users.

Issue Resolution: Establish processes for identifying and resolving issues with AI agents. This includes monitoring for errors, addressing user complaints, and implementing fixes promptly.

Best Practices for Implementing AI Agents

Implementing AI agents successfully requires following best practices to ensure smooth adoption and maximize benefits.

1.   Start Small and Scale Up

Pilot Projects: Begin with small-scale pilot projects to test the feasibility and impact of AI agents. Use the pilot to gather insights, identify challenges, and refine your approach.

Iterative Development: Use an iterative development approach to gradually scale up AI implementation. This allows you to make incremental improvements and adapt to changing requirements.

2.   Focus on User Experience

User-Centric Design: Design AI agents with the user experience in mind. Ensure that interactions are intuitive, seamless, and add value for users.

Feedback Mechanisms: Implement feedback mechanisms to gather user feedback and continuously improve AI agents. This includes surveys, user testing, and monitoring user interactions.

3.   Ensure Data Quality

Data Governance: Establish data governance practices to ensure data quality, accuracy, and consistency. This includes data validation, cleansing, and enrichment processes.

Data Privacy: Implement data privacy measures to protect user data and comply with regulations. This includes anonymizing data, obtaining user consent, and securing data storage.

4. Collaborate Across Teams

Cross-Functional Teams: Form cross-functional teams that include data scientists, engineers, domain experts, and business leaders. Collaboration ensures that AI agents are aligned with business goals and address real-world needs.

Stakeholder Engagement: Engage stakeholders throughout the implementation process to gather input, address concerns, and ensure buy-in. Regular communication and updates are key to maintaining stakeholder support.

5. Maintain Ethical Standards

Ethical AI: Develop and adhere to ethical guidelines for AI development and deployment. This includes ensuring fairness, transparency, accountability, and respect for user privacy.

Bias Mitigation: Actively work to identify and mitigate biases in AI models and data. Use diverse and representative datasets to train AI models and regularly audit for biases.

6. Continuous Improvement

Iterative Optimization: Continuously optimize AI agents based on performance data and user feedback. Regularly review and refine AI models, algorithms, and workflows.

Stay Informed: Stay informed about advancements in AI technology and best practices. Attend industry conferences, participate in professional networks, and invest in ongoing training for your team.

Key Resources and Tools

Implementing AI agents effectively requires access to a range of resources and tools that facilitate development, deployment, and management.

1. AI Development Platforms

Google AI Platform: Provides a suite of tools for building, training, and deploying machine learning models. It offers scalable infrastructure and integration with other Google Cloud services.

Microsoft Azure AI: Offers a comprehensive set of AI services and tools for developing intelligent applications. It includes Azure Machine Learning, Cognitive Services, and Bot Framework.

IBM Watson: Provides AI tools and services for building and deploying AI applications. Watson offers capabilities in natural language processing, machine learning, and data analysis.

OpenAI: Offers advanced AI models and tools, including the GPT series for natural language understanding and generation. OpenAI provides APIs and platforms to integrate cutting-edge AI capabilities into applications.

2. Machine Learning Frameworks

TensorFlow: An open-source machine learning framework developed by Google. It supports a wide range of applications, including neural networks and deep learning.

PyTorch: An open-source machine learning library developed by Facebook. It is known for its flexibility and ease of use, particularly for deep learning applications.

Scikit-learn: A popular open-source library for machine learning in Python. It provides simple and efficient tools for data analysis and modeling.

3. **Data Management Tools**

Apache Hadoop: An open-source framework for distributed storage and processing of large datasets. It supports the storage and analysis of big data.

Apache Spark: An open-source unified analytics engine for big data processing. It provides high-level APIs for machine learning and data processing.

Data Lakes: Platforms like Amazon S3, Google Cloud Storage, and Azure Data Lake store large volumes of raw data, enabling AI applications to access and process diverse datasets.

4. **Collaboration and Project Management Tools**

JIRA: A project management tool that supports agile development methodologies. It helps teams plan, track, and manage AI projects.

Confluence: A collaboration tool that enables teams to create, share, and collaborate on project documentation and knowledge bases.

GitHub: A platform for version control and collaboration. It allows teams to manage code repositories, track changes, and collaborate on AI development projects.

5. **Monitoring and Analytics Tools**

Prometheus: An open-source monitoring system that collects and stores metrics as time series data. It helps monitor the performance of AI systems.

Grafana: An open-source platform for monitoring and observability. It provides dashboards and visualization tools for analyzing metrics and performance data.

ELK Stack: A combination of Elasticsearch, Logstash, and Kibana used for searching, analyzing, and visualizing log data in real-time.

Building a Skilled Team

The successful implementation of AI agents depends on having a skilled team with expertise in AI, data science, and related fields.

1. **Key Roles and Responsibilities**

Data Scientists: Responsible for analyzing data, developing machine learning models, and interpreting results. They possess strong analytical and statistical skills.

AI Engineers: Focus on building and deploying AI systems. They have expertise in software development, machine learning frameworks, and cloud infrastructure.

Data Engineers: Handle the collection, storage, and processing of data. They ensure data pipelines are efficient and scalable, supporting AI applications.

Domain Experts: Provide subject matter expertise in the business domain where AI agents are deployed. They ensure AI solutions address real-world problems and meet business needs.

Project Managers: Oversee the planning, execution, and delivery of AI projects. They coordinate cross-functional teams and manage timelines, budgets, and resources.

2. Skills and Qualifications

Technical Skills: Team members should have expertise in machine learning, data analysis, programming languages (e.g., Python, R), and AI frameworks (e.g., TensorFlow, PyTorch).

Analytical Skills: Strong analytical skills are essential for understanding data, developing models, and interpreting results. Team members should be proficient in statistics and data analysis techniques.

Problem-Solving Skills: The ability to solve complex problems and develop innovative solutions is crucial for AI projects. Team members should be able to think critically and creatively.

Communication Skills: Effective communication is vital for collaborating with stakeholders, explaining technical concepts, and presenting findings. Team members should be able to convey complex information clearly and concisely.

3. Training and Development

Continuous Learning: Encourage team members to engage in continuous learning to stay updated with advancements in AI technology and best practices. This includes attending conferences, participating in online courses, and joining professional networks.

Certifications: Support team members in obtaining relevant certifications, such as Certified AI Practitioner, Microsoft Certified: Azure AI Engineer Associate, or Google Cloud Professional Data Engineer.

Workshops and Bootcamps: Organize workshops and bootcamps to provide hands-on training in AI tools, frameworks, and techniques. These sessions can help team members develop practical skills and knowledge.

4.   **Collaboration and Culture**

Cross-Functional Collaboration: Foster a collaborative environment where data scientists, engineers, domain experts, and business leaders work together. Cross-functional collaboration ensures AI solutions are aligned with business objectives and address real-world needs.

Innovation Culture: Promote a culture of innovation where team members are encouraged to experiment, take risks, and explore new ideas. This can lead to the development of creative and effective AI solutions.

Knowledge Sharing: Encourage knowledge sharing within the team and across the organization. Create forums, such as brown bag sessions, hackathons, and internal conferences, to facilitate the exchange of ideas and best practices.

Potential Challenges and How to Overcome Them

Implementing AI agents can present several challenges. Being aware of these challenges and knowing how to address them is crucial for success.

1.   **Data Challenges**

Data Quality: Ensuring high-quality data for training AI models can be challenging. Address this by implementing robust data governance practices and regularly cleaning and validating data.

Data Privacy: Protecting user data and complying with privacy regulations can be complex. Use privacy-enhancing technologies and ensure transparent data practices to build trust with users.

2. Technical Challenges

Integration Complexity: Integrating AI agents with existing systems can be technically challenging. Collaborate with IT and engineering teams to develop integration solutions and use middleware where necessary.

Scalability: Scaling AI systems to handle large volumes of interactions and data requires robust infrastructure. Invest in scalable cloud solutions and optimize AI models for performance.

3. Organizational Challenges

Resistance to Change: Employees and stakeholders may resist the adoption of AI due to fear of job displacement or unfamiliarity with the technology. Address this by providing training, communicating benefits, and involving them in the implementation process.

Resource Allocation: Implementing AI requires significant investment in terms of time, budget, and personnel. Build a strong business case to secure the necessary resources and allocate them effectively.

4. Ethical and Regulatory Challenges

Bias and Fairness: Ensuring that AI systems are fair and unbiased is an ongoing challenge. Regularly audit AI models for biases and use diverse datasets to train them.

Regulatory Compliance: Navigating the regulatory landscape for AI and data privacy requires careful planning. Stay informed about relevant regulations and ensure compliance through robust data practices.

Summary

Implementing AI agents in your business can provide significant benefits, including improved efficiency, cost savings, enhanced decision-making, and personalized experiences. Successful implementation requires understanding AI technology, aligning it with business objectives, and addressing practical considerations.

Key steps for implementing AI agents include planning and preparation, development and training, integration and deployment, and monitoring and maintenance. Following best practices, such as starting small, focusing on user experience, ensuring data quality, collaborating across teams, maintaining ethical standards, and continuous improvement, can help ensure successful adoption.

Potential challenges in implementing AI agents include data quality and privacy concerns, technical integration complexities, organizational resistance to change, and ethical and regulatory issues. Addressing these challenges through robust data governance, privacy-enhancing technologies, collaborative efforts, and staying informed about regulations can help overcome obstacles and achieve successful AI implementation.

By leveraging key resources and tools, building a skilled team, and taking a strategic and thoughtful approach, businesses can harness the power of AI to drive innovation, efficiency, and competitive advantage in an ever-evolving landscape.

Chapter 14: DIY AI Agents

AI is no longer confined to the realm of highly technical professionals. Today, a range of user-friendly tools makes it possible for non-programmers to create and deploy AI agents. This chapter explores essential tools for non-programmers, simple projects to get you started, and valuable learning resources.

Tools for Non-Programmers

Creating AI agents has become increasingly accessible due to various platforms and tools designed for users without extensive programming knowledge. Here are some of the most user-friendly and powerful tools available today:

1. Microsoft Power Platform

Power Automate: Automate workflows between apps and services. For example, you can set up a workflow that automatically collects data from emails and organizes it into a spreadsheet, or one that sends notifications when certain conditions are met in your data.

Power Apps: With Power Apps, you can build custom business apps with minimal coding. It provides templates and a drag-and-drop interface to create apps that can connect to your data sources.

Power Virtual Agents: This tool helps you create chatbots using a graphical interface. You can design conversation flows, integrate them with other services, and deploy them on websites or social media platforms.

2. Google Cloud AutoML

AutoML Vision: Allows you to train custom machine learning models for image recognition with minimal effort. You can upload your images, label them, and let AutoML Vision do the rest.

AutoML Natural Language: Enables you to build models for sentiment analysis, entity recognition, and text classification by simply uploading and labeling your text data.

AutoML Tables: Simplifies the process of building machine learning models on structured data. You can upload your CSV files, select target columns, and AutoML Tables will train and deploy a model for you.

3.   **IBM Watson Studio**

Watson Studio: Provides a suite of tools for building, training, and deploying machine learning models with a visual drag-and-drop interface. You can collaborate with others, use pre-built models, or create your own.

Watson Assistant: Helps you create conversational AI applications that understand natural language and interact with users. You can design intents, entities, and dialog flows without coding.

4.   **OpenAI**

ChatGPT: OpenAI's ChatGPT allows you to create conversational AI agents capable of engaging in human-like dialogue. You can use it for customer support, content creation, or any scenario where natural language interaction is beneficial.

DALL-E: This tool can generate images from textual descriptions. It's useful for creative projects where you need custom illustrations or visual content generated on the fly.

5.   **Teachable Machine by Google**

Teachable Machine: A web-based tool that lets you create machine learning models for image, sound, and pose recognition without any coding. You simply upload or capture data, train the model, and integrate it into your applications using export options for TensorFlow.js, P5.js, and more.

6. Lobe by Microsoft

Lobe: An easy-to-use tool for training image classification models. It provides a simple visual interface for labeling data and training models. Once trained, you can export the model for use in various applications.

7. Dialogflow by Google

Dialogflow: A natural language understanding platform for designing conversational interfaces for apps, websites, and bots. It supports voice and text-based conversational interfaces and integrates with various platforms such as Google Assistant, Amazon Alexa, and Facebook Messenger.

8. Anthropic Claude

Claude: An AI assistant developed by Anthropic, known for its reliability and ease of customization. It can handle various conversational and text processing tasks.

9. Adobe Firefly

Firefly: A generative AI tool integrated into Adobe's suite. It allows you to create images, text effects, and more using simple text prompts. It's particularly useful for creative professionals looking to enhance their workflow with AI.

10. Nyckel

Nyckel: A no-code AI tool for text and image classification. It allows you to build models quickly and easily by uploading data and defining classes.

Simple Projects to Get You Started

To help you get started with DIY AI, here are some beginner-friendly projects using the tools mentioned above:

1. Creating a Chatbot with Microsoft Power Virtual Agents

Steps:

1. **Sign In**: Access Microsoft Power Virtual Agents through the Microsoft Power Platform portal.
2. **Create a Bot**: Use the graphical interface to design conversation flows. Start with a simple greeting message and add triggers for different intents, such as answering FAQs or providing product information.
3. **Integration**: Integrate your bot with platforms like Microsoft Teams or embed it on your website.
4. **Testing**: Use the built-in testing environment to simulate interactions and refine your bot's responses.
5. **Deployment**: Deploy your bot and monitor its performance using the provided analytics tools.

Use Case: Create a customer service bot that answers frequently asked questions, provides product information, and assists with basic troubleshooting.

2. Building an Image Classifier with Teachable Machine

Steps:

1. **Choose a Project**: Go to the Teachable Machine website and select the "Image Project" option.
2. **Upload Data**: Upload images or use your webcam to capture training data for different classes. For example, you could train a model to recognize different types of fruits.

3. **Train the Model**: Click the "Train Model" button to start the training process.
4. **Test the Model**: Use new images to test the model's predictions.
5. **Export the Model**: Export the trained model for use in web applications or other platforms.

Use Case: Create a simple image classifier that can identify different types of objects, such as fruits, animals, or everyday items.

3.   Developing a Sentiment Analysis Tool with Google Cloud AutoML Natural Language

Steps:

1. **Sign In**: Access Google Cloud Platform and navigate to AutoML Natural Language.
2. **Create a Dataset**: Upload text samples labeled with their respective sentiments (positive, negative, neutral).
3. **Train the Model**: Select the training options and initiate the training process.
4. **Evaluate the Model**: Use the provided metrics to evaluate the model's performance.
5. **Deploy the Model**: Deploy the model and use it to analyze the sentiment of new text inputs.

Use Case: Build a tool that analyzes customer reviews or social media posts to determine the overall sentiment and gain insights into customer opinions.

4.   Creating a Custom Voice Assistant with IBM Watson Assistant

Steps:

1. **Sign In**: Access IBM Watson Assistant and create a new assistant.
2. **Define Intents and Entities**: Identify the different intents (user goals) and entities (specific pieces of information) your assistant should recognize.
3. **Build Dialog Flows**: Design conversation flows to handle different types of interactions. Use the visual editor to add responses and actions.
4. **Integration**: Integrate the assistant with voice input/output using IBM Watson Text to Speech and Speech to Text services.
5. **Testing and Deployment**: Test the assistant's responses and deploy it on various platforms.

Use Case: Develop a voice assistant that can help users with tasks such as setting reminders, providing weather updates, or answering general knowledge questions.

5. **Implementing an Object Detection Model with Lobe**

Steps:

1. **Download Lobe**: Install the Lobe application on your computer.
2. **Label Images**: Import images and label them for the objects you want to detect.
3. **Train the Model**: Follow the guided steps in Lobe to train the model.
4. **Test the Model**: Use new images to test the model's accuracy.
5. **Export the Model**: Export the model for use in applications using the provided export options.

Use Case: Create an object detection system that can identify items in real-time through a webcam, such as identifying different types of plants or monitoring the presence of certain objects in a room.

Learning Resources

To further your knowledge and skills in AI, here are some valuable learning resources that can help you stay updated with the latest advancements and best practices in AI development.

1. Online Courses and Tutorials

Coursera: Offers a wide range of AI and machine learning courses from top universities and companies. For example, Stanford's "Machine Learning" course by Andrew Ng provides a comprehensive introduction to the field.

edX: Provides courses on AI and machine learning from institutions like MIT, Harvard, and Microsoft. Courses like "Artificial Intelligence: Principles and Techniques" by Stanford cover foundational concepts and practical applications.

Udacity: Features Nanodegree programs focused on AI and machine learning. The "Artificial Intelligence Nanodegree" and "Machine Learning Engineer Nanodegree" provide in-depth knowledge and hands-on experience.

2. Books

"Artificial Intelligence: A Modern Approach" by Stuart Russell and Peter Norvig: A comprehensive textbook covering the fundamentals of AI, including search algorithms, machine learning, and natural language processing.

"Hands-On Machine Learning with Scikit-Learn, Keras, and TensorFlow" by Aurélien Géron: A practical guide to implementing machine learning algorithms using popular Python libraries.

"Deep Learning" by Ian Goodfellow, Yoshua Bengio, and Aaron Courville: An in-depth exploration of deep learning techniques and their applications.

3. Websites and Blogs

Towards Data Science: A popular blog on Medium that features articles, tutorials, and case studies on AI, machine learning, and data science.

KDnuggets: A leading site for data science, machine learning, and AI news, resources, and tutorials.

AI Trends: A website that covers the latest trends, research, and applications in AI across various industries.

4. YouTube Channels

3Blue1Brown: A YouTube channel that provides visually engaging explanations of mathematical concepts, including those related to AI and machine learning.

Sentdex: Offers tutorials on Python programming, machine learning, and AI, with practical examples and projects.

Siraj Raval: Features tutorials and discussions on AI, machine learning, and blockchain technology, aimed at making complex topics accessible to beginners.

5. Communities and Forums

Reddit: Subreddits such as r/MachineLearning, r/artificial, and r/datascience are great places to ask questions, share knowledge, and stay updated with the latest developments in AI.

Stack Overflow: A community of developers and data scientists where you can ask technical questions and find answers related to AI and machine learning.

Kaggle: A platform for data science competitions that also offers datasets, tutorials, and a community of data scientists and AI enthusiasts.

6.   **Conferences and Meetups**

NeurIPS (Conference on Neural Information Processing Systems): A leading AI conference that covers the latest research and advancements in machine learning and AI.

ICML (International Conference on Machine Learning): An annual conference that brings together researchers and practitioners in the field of machine learning.

Meetup: Join local AI and machine learning meetups to network with professionals, attend workshops, and participate in discussions.

Summary

Creating AI agents is now accessible to non-programmers thanks to a range of user-friendly tools and platforms. This chapter provided an overview of essential tools, simple projects to get you started, and valuable learning resources. Leveraging these resources and experimenting with DIY AI projects can empower you to harness the power of AI for personal and professional applications.

Chapter 15: Collaborating with AI Experts

Collaborating with AI experts can significantly enhance your ability to implement and leverage AI technologies effectively. Whether you are looking to augment your team with specialized skills, tap into external expertise, or manage complex AI projects, finding the right partners and consultants is crucial. This chapter provides a comprehensive guide to collaborating with AI experts, covering key aspects such as finding the right partners, working with consultants and developers, and managing AI projects.

Finding the Right Partners

Finding the right AI partners involves identifying individuals or organizations that possess the expertise, experience, and resources needed to support your AI initiatives. This process requires careful consideration and strategic planning to ensure that you select partners who can contribute effectively to your AI projects.

Define Your Needs and Goals

Before beginning your search for AI partners, it's essential to have a clear understanding of your needs and goals. Start by assessing your internal capabilities to determine the skills and resources you currently have within your organization. Identify any gaps in knowledge, expertise, or technology that need to be filled by external partners. Set specific objectives for your AI projects, such as improving customer service, optimizing operations, or developing new products. Having clear, well-defined objectives will guide your search for the right partners and help you articulate your requirements effectively.

Research Potential Partners

Conduct thorough research to identify potential partners who meet your criteria. Here are key areas to focus on:

1.   **Industry Expertise**: Look for partners with proven experience in your industry. They should understand the unique challenges and opportunities within your sector. For example, if you are in healthcare, a partner with experience in medical data analytics would be valuable. Review their past projects and case studies to gauge their expertise.

2.   **Technical Expertise**: Ensure that potential partners have strong technical expertise in AI, machine learning, and data science. Evaluate their proficiency in relevant technologies and tools. Check if they have certifications or affiliations with recognized AI institutions.

3.   **Reputation and References**: Reputation is crucial when selecting a partner. Seek references from their previous clients to understand their track record. Read reviews and testimonials to get insights into their reliability and quality of work. Industry networks and professional associations can also provide valuable feedback on potential partners.

Engage with AI Communities and Networks

Networking within AI communities and professional associations can help you identify potential partners. Here are some ways to engage with these communities:

1.   **Professional Associations**: Join AI-related professional associations such as the Association for the Advancement of Artificial Intelligence (AAAI) or the International Association for Artificial Intelligence and Law (IAAIL). These associations often have directories or forums where you can connect with AI experts and companies.

2.   **Conferences and Events**: Attend AI conferences, workshops, and meetups. Events like the Conference on Neural Information Processing Systems (NeurIPS) or the International Conference on Machine Learning (ICML) are excellent opportunities to meet

potential partners, learn about the latest trends, and network with industry leaders.

3.   **Online Communities**: Participate in online AI communities and forums such as Reddit's r/MachineLearning, Stack Overflow, or AI-focused LinkedIn groups. These platforms allow you to engage with AI professionals, ask questions, and seek recommendations.

Evaluate Cultural Fit

Cultural fit is an often-overlooked but critical factor in successful partnerships. Ensure that potential partners share similar values and work ethics. A good cultural fit can lead to more effective collaboration and smoother project execution. Consider the following aspects:

1.   **Alignment of Values**: Assess whether the partner's values align with your organization's mission and vision. This includes their approach to innovation, quality, and customer satisfaction.

2.   **Communication and Collaboration**: Evaluate their communication style and collaboration approach. Effective communication is essential for successful partnerships. Partners who are open, transparent, and responsive are likely to contribute positively to the project.

3.   **Work Ethic and Commitment**: Gauge their work ethic and commitment to project goals. Partners who demonstrate dedication, reliability, and a proactive attitude are more likely to deliver successful outcomes.

Assess Financial Stability and Scalability

Financial stability and scalability are important considerations when selecting a partner. Ensure that the potential partner has the financial health to sustain the project and the capability to scale operations if needed.

1.   **Financial Health**: Review the financial statements of the potential partner to assess their financial stability. This includes evaluating their revenue, profit margins, and investment in technology and innovation.
2.   **Scalability**: Consider the partner's ability to scale their operations to meet your project's demands. This includes their capacity to handle larger volumes of work, expand their team, and invest in additional resources if required.

Conduct Due Diligence

Due diligence is a critical step in selecting the right AI partner. This involves a thorough investigation of the partner's background, capabilities, and track record. Here are some steps to conduct due diligence:

1.   **Background Check**: Perform a comprehensive background check on the partner. This includes verifying their credentials, certifications, and affiliations with industry bodies.
2.   **Legal and Compliance**: Ensure that the partner complies with relevant legal and regulatory requirements. This includes data protection laws, industry standards, and ethical guidelines for AI development.
3.   **Security and Risk Management**: Evaluate the partner's security measures and risk management practices. Ensure that they have robust protocols in place to protect data and mitigate risks associated with AI projects.

Engage in Pilot Projects

Before committing to a long-term partnership, consider engaging the potential partner in a pilot project. This allows you to assess their capabilities, work ethic, and cultural fit in a real-world scenario. A successful pilot project can build confidence and provide valuable insights into how well the partnership will work on larger, more complex projects.

Negotiate Terms and Agreements

Once you have identified the right partner, negotiate the terms and agreements of the partnership. This includes defining the scope of work, deliverables, timelines, and performance metrics. Ensure that the contract includes clauses for confidentiality, intellectual property rights, dispute resolution, and termination conditions.

Foster Long-Term Relationships

Building a long-term relationship with your AI partner can lead to ongoing collaboration and continuous improvement. Foster a partnership based on mutual trust, respect, and shared goals. Regularly review the partnership's progress and make adjustments as needed to ensure continued success.

Working with Consultants and Developers

Once you have identified potential partners, the next step is to effectively work with AI consultants and developers. Successful collaboration with these experts involves several key components: clearly defining roles and responsibilities, developing a detailed project plan, fostering collaboration and knowledge sharing, managing change and expectations, and ensuring continuous communication and feedback.

Define Roles and Responsibilities

To start, it is crucial to establish clear roles and responsibilities for each party involved in the project. This involves specifying deliverables, timelines, and performance metrics to ensure that everyone understands their accountability for specific tasks and outcomes. Having a well-defined structure helps in setting the right expectations and avoids overlaps or gaps in responsibilities.

1. **Set Clear Expectations**: Begin by outlining what you expect from the consultants and developers. This includes the scope of work, key deliverables, and deadlines. Make sure these expectations are documented and agreed upon by all parties.
2. **Establish Ownership**: Assign ownership for different aspects of the project. This includes not only technical tasks but also communication, documentation, and stakeholder management. Each team member should know their specific role and responsibilities.

Develop a Detailed Project Plan

A comprehensive project plan is essential for guiding the AI development process. This plan should detail the project scope, objectives, milestones, and resources required.

1. **Scope and Objectives**: Clearly define the project's scope and objectives. This includes outlining what the project will achieve and the boundaries within which it will operate. Ensure that these objectives are specific, measurable, achievable, relevant, and time-bound (SMART).
2. **Milestones and Timelines**: Break the project into manageable milestones with specific deliverables and deadlines. This helps in tracking progress and ensures that the project stays on schedule. Use project management tools like Gantt charts to visualize the timeline and dependencies.
3. **Resource Allocation**: Identify the resources required for the project, including personnel, technology, and budget. Ensure that these resources are allocated appropriately and that there are contingency plans for any unforeseen challenges.

Foster Collaboration and Knowledge Sharing

Collaboration between your internal team and the external consultants or developers is crucial for the success of the project. Fostering an environment of open communication and knowledge sharing helps in building a cohesive team.

1.   **Regular Meetings**: Schedule regular meetings to discuss progress, challenges, and next steps. These meetings can be daily stand-ups, weekly reviews, or milestone check-ins. Use these sessions to align on priorities and address any issues promptly.
2.   **Joint Workshops**: Conduct joint workshops and brainstorming sessions to encourage creative problem-solving and innovation. These sessions help in leveraging the collective expertise of the team and can lead to better solutions.
3.   **Shared Workspaces**: Utilize shared workspaces and collaboration tools like Slack, Microsoft Teams, or Trello to facilitate real-time communication and collaboration. These platforms enable team members to share updates, files, and feedback easily.
4.   **Documentation and Knowledge Transfer**: Ensure that all project-related knowledge is documented and shared with the internal team. This includes technical documentation, user manuals, and training materials. Conduct knowledge transfer sessions to help your team understand the AI models, tools, and processes used in the project.

Manage Change and Expectations

AI projects are often complex and may require adjustments along the way. Managing change and setting realistic expectations are critical for maintaining project momentum and stakeholder trust.

1.   **Flexibility**: Be prepared for changes and adjustments throughout the project. AI projects can be unpredictable, and

flexibility is often needed to address unforeseen challenges. Have a change management process in place to handle these adjustments smoothly.

2.   **Expectation Management**: Set realistic expectations with stakeholders about the potential outcomes and timelines of the AI project. Communicate the inherent uncertainties and complexities of AI development and ensure that stakeholders understand the iterative nature of the process.

3.   **Regular Updates**: Keep stakeholders informed about the project's progress through regular updates and reports. Transparency helps build trust and ensures alignment with business goals. Use dashboards and reporting tools to provide real-time insights into project status and performance.

Ensure Continuous Communication and Feedback

Continuous communication and feedback are vital for the success of AI projects. They help in identifying and addressing issues early, ensuring that the project stays on track.

1.   **Feedback Loops**: Establish feedback loops where team members and stakeholders can provide input and suggestions. This feedback should be incorporated into the project to ensure it meets their needs and expectations.

2.   **Issue Resolution**: Have a process in place for resolving issues and conflicts promptly. Encourage open and honest communication to surface problems early and address them before they escalate.

3.   **Performance Reviews**: Conduct regular performance reviews to evaluate the effectiveness of the collaboration and the progress of the project. Use these reviews to identify areas for improvement and make necessary adjustments.

By focusing on these aspects, you can create a productive and collaborative environment that maximizes the expertise of AI consultants and developers, ensuring the successful implementation of your AI projects.

Managing AI Projects

Effective project management is critical for the success of AI initiatives. Key strategies for managing AI projects include agile project management, risk management, performance metrics and evaluation, stakeholder engagement, data management and quality assurance, ethical considerations and compliance, scalability and deployment, and continuous improvement and learning.

Agile Project Management

Agile methodologies are highly effective for managing AI projects. They involve iterative development, frequent testing, and continuous feedback. Agile approaches help accommodate changes and improve the project's adaptability. Breaking down the project into manageable sprints with specific deliverables and goals, and conducting regular sprint reviews to assess progress and make necessary adjustments, is key to successful project management.

Risk Management

Risk management is another crucial aspect of managing AI projects. Identifying potential risks associated with the AI project, such as data quality issues, technical challenges, or regulatory compliance, is the first step. Developing a risk management plan to mitigate these risks and continuously monitoring the project for emerging risks is essential. Implementing mitigation strategies and contingency plans to address issues promptly ensures that risks are managed effectively.

Performance Metrics and Evaluation

Defining clear performance metrics is essential for evaluating the success of the AI project. Establish metrics such as accuracy, efficiency, user satisfaction, and business impact. Regularly evaluate the project's performance against these metrics to make data-driven decisions and improve the project's outcomes.

Stakeholder Engagement

Engaging stakeholders throughout the project is key to ensuring alignment with business goals. Keeping stakeholders informed about the project's progress through regular updates and reports builds trust and ensures that the project remains aligned with business objectives. Creating a feedback loop where stakeholders can provide input and suggestions, and incorporating their feedback into the project, ensures it meets their needs and expectations.

Data Management and Quality Assurance

Effective data management and quality assurance are critical for the success of AI projects. Ensuring that data is collected, cleaned, and prepared accurately is essential for training effective AI models. Regularly validating and testing data to maintain its accuracy and relevance, and implementing automated tools and processes to detect and correct errors, ensures data quality.

Ethical Considerations and Compliance

Addressing ethical considerations and compliance is also important. Ensuring that AI models are fair and unbiased by using diverse datasets and regularly auditing models for bias is crucial. Ensuring compliance with relevant regulations and standards, and staying informed about legal requirements related to data privacy, security, and AI ethics, is essential for maintaining ethical AI practices.

Scalability and Deployment

Designing AI systems with scalability in mind ensures that the infrastructure can handle increased loads and adapt to growing demands. Developing a clear deployment strategy that includes testing in different environments, monitoring performance, and rolling out updates smoothly is key to successful deployment.

Continuous Improvement and Learning

Encouraging continuous improvement and learning is essential for the long-term success of AI projects. Conducting a thorough review after project completion to identify successes, challenges, and areas for improvement, and documenting lessons learned and best practices, ensures ongoing improvement. Encouraging continuous learning and improvement by keeping up with AI advancements, updating models and systems, and incorporating new techniques and technologies, ensures that the AI system remains effective and up-to-date.

Summary

Collaborating with AI experts can greatly enhance your organization's AI capabilities and ensure the success of your AI initiatives. By finding the right partners, effectively working with consultants and developers, and implementing robust project management practices, you can harness the power of AI to drive innovation, efficiency, and competitive advantage. Effective project management, including agile methodologies, risk management, performance evaluation, stakeholder engagement, data management, ethical considerations, scalability, and continuous improvement, is critical for the success of AI projects.

Chapter 16: AI Agents and the Future of Work

As AI agents become more integrated into various aspects of business and daily life, their impact on the workforce is expected to grow significantly. This chapter explores how AI agents will redefine jobs and roles, the skills needed for an AI-driven economy, and how to prepare for the future workplace.

Redefining Jobs and Roles

The Shift in Job Functions

AI agents are set to transform job functions across industries. Automation and intelligent systems will take over repetitive and mundane tasks, allowing human workers to focus on more complex and creative aspects of their roles. This shift will affect a wide range of jobs, from administrative roles to technical positions.

Administrative and Clerical Jobs

Administrative and clerical jobs are among the most impacted by AI. Tasks such as data entry, scheduling, and basic customer service are increasingly being handled by AI agents.

- **Data Entry and Management**: AI systems can automate data entry tasks by extracting information from documents and populating databases. Optical Character Recognition (OCR) and Natural Language Processing (NLP) technologies enable AI to accurately read and interpret text from various sources, significantly reducing the need for manual data entry.
- **Scheduling and Coordination**: AI-powered virtual assistants, like Google Assistant and Amazon Alexa, can manage calendars, schedule meetings, and send reminders. These tools streamline administrative workflows, ensuring that appointments are managed efficiently and reducing the administrative burden on human staff.
- **Customer Service**: Basic customer service tasks, such as answering frequently asked questions and resolving simple issues, are increasingly handled by AI chatbots. These chatbots use NLP to

understand and respond to customer inquiries, providing instant support and freeing up human agents to handle more complex queries.

Manufacturing and Production

In manufacturing, AI agents are enhancing production processes through predictive maintenance, quality control, and supply chain optimization. Robots and AI systems can perform repetitive tasks with precision, reducing errors and increasing efficiency.

• **Predictive Maintenance**: AI-powered predictive maintenance systems analyze data from sensors and machinery to predict when equipment is likely to fail. By identifying potential issues before they occur, these systems help prevent unplanned downtime and extend the lifespan of equipment.

• **Quality Control**: AI systems equipped with computer vision can inspect products for defects more accurately and consistently than human inspectors. These systems can identify imperfections at a microscopic level, ensuring that only high-quality products reach the market.

• **Supply Chain Optimization**: AI agents optimize supply chain operations by analyzing demand patterns, inventory levels, and transportation routes. Machine learning algorithms can predict demand fluctuations and adjust inventory levels accordingly, reducing waste and improving efficiency.

Healthcare

AI agents are revolutionizing healthcare by assisting in diagnostics, patient monitoring, and personalized treatment plans. AI systems can analyze medical images, predict disease outbreaks, and manage patient records, allowing healthcare professionals to focus on patient care and advanced medical procedures.

• **Diagnostics**: AI systems, such as IBM Watson for Oncology, analyze vast amounts of medical data to assist in diagnosing diseases. These systems can identify patterns and correlations that might be missed by human doctors, leading to more accurate diagnoses.

• **Patient Monitoring**: Wearable devices and AI-powered monitoring systems continuously track patients' vital signs and health metrics. These systems can alert healthcare providers to any abnormal readings, enabling timely interventions and reducing the risk of complications.

• **Personalized Treatment Plans**: AI systems analyze patient data, including genetic information, to develop personalized treatment plans. These tailored approaches can improve treatment outcomes and reduce the likelihood of adverse reactions.

Finance

In the financial sector, AI agents are automating tasks such as fraud detection, risk assessment, and customer service. AI-powered chatbots can handle customer inquiries, while machine learning algorithms analyze transaction data to detect fraudulent activities.

• **Fraud Detection**: AI systems analyze transaction data to identify unusual patterns that may indicate fraudulent activity. Machine learning algorithms continuously learn from new data, improving their ability to detect and prevent fraud.

• **Risk Assessment**: AI-powered risk assessment tools evaluate the creditworthiness of individuals and businesses by analyzing a wide range of data points. These tools provide more accurate and objective assessments than traditional methods, reducing the risk for financial institutions.

• **Customer Service**: AI chatbots and virtual assistants handle routine customer inquiries, such as balance inquiries and transaction history requests. These tools provide instant responses, improving customer satisfaction and freeing up human agents to handle more complex issues.

Emerging Roles and New Job Opportunities

While some jobs will be automated, AI will also create new roles and opportunities. As industries evolve, there will be a growing demand for skills that complement AI technologies.

AI Trainers and Technicians

AI Trainers

AI systems require continuous training to improve their accuracy and effectiveness. AI trainers play a crucial role in this process by providing the necessary data inputs and refining algorithms. This involves curating datasets, labeling data, and feeding this information into AI models to help them learn and improve. AI trainers also evaluate the performance of AI systems and make necessary adjustments to the training process.

For example, in natural language processing applications, AI trainers might work on improving a virtual assistant's ability to understand and respond to user queries by providing examples of various ways a question might be asked and the appropriate responses.

AI Technicians

AI technicians are responsible for the maintenance and troubleshooting of AI systems. They ensure that AI tools and technologies are functioning correctly and efficiently. This role involves monitoring AI system performance, diagnosing issues, and implementing solutions to technical problems. AI technicians work closely with data scientists and engineers to integrate AI technologies into existing systems and processes.

In manufacturing, AI technicians might oversee robotic systems on the production line, ensuring they are operating as expected and addressing any mechanical or software issues that arise.

Data Scientists and Analysts

Data Scientists

Data scientists are in high demand as organizations increasingly rely on data-driven insights to make informed decisions. These professionals collect, analyze, and interpret large datasets to uncover patterns and trends that can inform business strategies. Data scientists use a variety of tools and techniques, including machine learning algorithms, statistical analysis, and data visualization, to extract valuable insights from data.

For instance, a data scientist in the healthcare industry might analyze patient data to identify risk factors for certain diseases and develop predictive models to improve patient outcomes.

Data Analysts

Data analysts focus on interpreting data and turning it into actionable information. They work with datasets to identify trends, generate reports, and provide insights that help organizations make data-driven decisions. Data analysts use tools such as SQL, Excel, and data visualization software to process and present data in a meaningful way.

In retail, data analysts might analyze sales data to determine which products are performing well and identify opportunities for inventory optimization and marketing strategies.

AI Ethicists and Compliance Officers

AI Ethicists

As AI systems become more pervasive, ethical considerations are becoming increasingly important. AI ethicists ensure that AI technologies are developed and used responsibly, addressing concerns such as bias, fairness, transparency, and accountability. These professionals work to establish ethical guidelines and standards for AI development and deployment, ensuring that AI systems do not perpetuate harmful biases or infringe on privacy rights.

For example, an AI ethicist might evaluate a facial recognition system to ensure it does not disproportionately misidentify individuals based on race or gender.

Compliance Officers

Compliance officers oversee adherence to legal and regulatory standards related to AI and data usage. They ensure that organizations comply with laws and regulations governing data protection, privacy, and AI ethics. Compliance officers develop policies and procedures to ensure that AI systems are used in a manner that complies with relevant regulations and industry standards.

In the financial sector, a compliance officer might ensure that AI algorithms used for credit scoring are fair and do not discriminate against certain demographic groups.

Human-AI Collaboration Specialists

As AI systems become integral to various workflows, there is a growing need for specialists who can facilitate effective collaboration between humans and AI agents. Human-AI collaboration specialists focus on integrating AI technologies into the workplace, ensuring that employees can work seamlessly with AI tools and technologies. They design workflows that leverage the strengths of both humans and AI, enhancing productivity and efficiency.

For example, in customer service, a human-AI collaboration specialist might develop a system where AI chatbots handle routine inquiries, while human agents focus on more complex issues that require empathy and problem-solving skills.

Change Management and Integration Experts

These professionals help organizations manage the transition to AI-enhanced workflows. They develop strategies for implementing AI technologies, training employees, and ensuring that the integration process is smooth and effective. Change management experts work to minimize disruption and maximize the benefits of AI adoption.

In the logistics industry, an integration expert might oversee the implementation of an AI-driven route optimization system, ensuring that employees are trained to use the new technology effectively.

Skills for the AI-Driven Economy

As AI technologies become more prevalent, the skills required in the workforce are also evolving. Professionals will need a combination of technical expertise and soft skills to thrive in the AI-driven economy.

Technical Skills

Machine Learning and AI

Understanding the principles of machine learning and AI is essential for developing and maintaining AI systems. This includes knowledge of algorithms, neural networks, and deep learning techniques.

Data Science and Analytics

Proficiency in data science and analytics is crucial for interpreting data and deriving actionable insights. Skills in statistical analysis, data visualization, and data mining will be valuable.

Programming and Software Development

Familiarity with programming languages such as Python, R, and Java is important for building AI applications. Software development skills will enable professionals to create, test, and deploy AI solutions.

Soft Skills

Critical Thinking and Problem-Solving

The ability to think critically and solve complex problems will be essential as AI systems handle more routine tasks. Professionals will need to analyze situations, identify challenges, and develop innovative solutions. This skill involves not just identifying problems but also understanding their root causes and thinking creatively to find effective solutions. As AI takes over repetitive tasks, the human ability to approach problems from various angles and devise unique solutions will become even more valuable.

Creativity and Innovation

Creativity will be a key differentiator in the AI-driven economy. Professionals who can generate new ideas and approaches will be valuable in developing unique AI applications and improving existing systems. Creativity involves thinking outside the box and applying knowledge in novel ways to solve problems and create value. This skill will be particularly important in roles that require designing AI-driven products, services, and experiences that meet the evolving needs of users.

Communication and Collaboration

Effective communication and collaboration skills will be crucial for working with diverse teams and integrating AI technologies into various workflows. Professionals will need to articulate their ideas clearly and work collaboratively with others. This includes the ability to explain complex technical concepts to non-technical stakeholders, facilitate discussions, and build consensus. Collaboration will be key in multidisciplinary teams where members bring different expertise and perspectives to the table.

Adaptability and Lifelong Learning

The rapid pace of technological change requires professionals to be adaptable and committed to lifelong learning. Staying updated with the latest AI advancements and continuously upgrading skills will be necessary for career growth. This involves being open to new ideas, willing to learn new technologies, and adapting to new ways of working. Lifelong learning is essential for keeping skills relevant and being able to take advantage of new opportunities as they arise.

Educational Pathways and Training Programs

To prepare for the AI-driven economy, individuals can pursue various educational pathways and training programs.

University Degrees

Degrees in computer science, data science, and engineering provide a solid foundation in AI and related fields. Many universities offer specialized programs in AI and machine learning. These programs cover fundamental concepts and advanced techniques, providing students with the knowledge and skills needed to develop and implement AI systems.

Online Courses and Certifications

Online platforms such as Coursera, edX, and Udacity offer courses and certifications in AI, machine learning, and data science. These programs provide flexibility for learners to study at their own pace. Courses are often developed in collaboration with leading universities and industry experts, ensuring that the content is up-to-date and relevant.

Bootcamps and Workshops

Intensive bootcamps and workshops offer hands-on training in AI and data science. These programs often focus on practical skills and real-world applications. Bootcamps are typically short-term, immersive programs that provide comprehensive training on specific topics. Workshops may be shorter and more focused on particular skills or technologies.

Corporate Training Programs

Many organizations provide in-house training programs to upskill their employees in AI and related technologies. These programs are tailored to the specific needs of the company and its industry. Corporate training programs can include workshops, seminars, and ongoing learning opportunities, ensuring that employees stay current with the latest advancements.

Preparing for the Future Workplace

Embracing Change and Innovation

Preparing for the future workplace requires embracing change and fostering a culture of innovation. Organizations must be proactive in adopting AI technologies and adapting their business models to leverage these advancements.

Cultivating an Innovative Mindset

Encourage employees to think creatively and explore new ideas. Foster a culture that rewards experimentation and innovation, allowing teams to take calculated risks and learn from failures. This can be achieved by creating innovation labs, offering incentives for innovative ideas, and promoting a mindset that values curiosity and continuous improvement.

Investing in Research and Development

Allocate resources to research and development (R&D) to stay ahead of technological trends. Investing in R&D enables organizations to develop cutting-edge AI solutions and maintain a competitive edge. This includes funding for internal projects, collaborations with academic institutions, and partnerships with technology companies.

Agile and Flexible Work Practices

Implement agile methodologies and flexible work practices to adapt to changing market conditions. Agile frameworks such as Scrum and Kanban promote iterative development and continuous improvement. Flexible work practices, including remote work and flexible hours, can help attract and retain top talent.

Building a Collaborative Work Environment

A collaborative work environment is essential for maximizing the potential of AI technologies. Effective collaboration between humans and AI agents can lead to improved productivity and innovation.

Integrating AI into Workflows

Seamlessly integrate AI tools into existing workflows to enhance efficiency. For example, AI-powered analytics can provide real-time insights to support decision-making processes. This requires identifying opportunities where AI can add value and designing workflows that incorporate AI capabilities.

Promoting Cross-Functional Teams

Encourage cross-functional collaboration by forming teams with diverse skill sets. Cross-functional teams can leverage different perspectives to develop comprehensive AI solutions. This involves breaking down silos and fostering a collaborative culture where team members from different departments work together towards common goals.

Enhancing Communication Channels

Use collaboration tools such as Slack, Microsoft Teams, and Zoom to facilitate communication and knowledge sharing. These tools enable teams to stay connected and work together effectively, regardless of their location. Clear and open communication channels are essential for ensuring that everyone is on the same page and that information flows freely within the organization.

Fostering Continuous Learning and Development

Continuous learning and development are crucial for staying competitive in the AI-driven economy. Organizations must provide opportunities for employees to upskill and reskill regularly.

Creating Learning Pathways

Develop clear learning pathways that outline the skills and competencies needed for various roles. Provide access to training resources, including online courses, workshops, and mentorship programs. Learning pathways should be aligned with career development plans, helping employees to advance in their careers while acquiring new skills.

Encouraging Lifelong Learning

Promote a culture of lifelong learning by encouraging employees to pursue new knowledge and skills. Recognize and reward continuous learning efforts to motivate employees. This can include offering financial support for education, providing time off for learning activities, and celebrating learning achievements.

Implementing Mentorship Programs

Establish mentorship programs where experienced professionals can guide and support less experienced colleagues. Mentorship fosters knowledge transfer and helps employees navigate their career paths. Mentors can provide valuable insights, share experiences, and offer advice on career development and skill acquisition.

Adapting Leadership and Management Styles

Leadership and management styles must evolve to support the integration of AI technologies and the changing nature of work.

Empowering Teams

Shift from traditional hierarchical management to a more decentralized approach that empowers teams. Provide autonomy and decision-making authority to teams, allowing them to respond quickly to changes. Empowered teams are more engaged, motivated, and capable of driving innovation.

Developing Emotional Intelligence

Leaders must develop emotional intelligence to effectively manage diverse teams and foster a positive work environment. Emotional intelligence helps leaders understand and address the needs and concerns of their employees. This involves being empathetic, self-aware, and adept at managing relationships.

Leading by Example

Demonstrate a commitment to innovation and continuous learning by staying informed about AI advancements and participating in training programs. Leading by example inspires employees to embrace change and pursue growth opportunities. Leaders who actively engage in learning and development set a positive tone for the organization.

Summary

AI agents are poised to redefine the future of work by transforming job functions, creating new roles, and driving demand for new skills. As organizations prepare for this AI-driven future, they must focus on fostering a culture of innovation, building collaborative work environments, and promoting continuous learning and development. By adapting leadership styles and embracing change, businesses can harness the power of AI to drive growth, efficiency, and competitive advantage.

Chapter 17: AI Agents and Society

AI agents are rapidly transforming society, bringing about significant social and cultural impacts, raising important questions about inequality and accessibility, and necessitating thoughtful policy and regulation. This chapter delves into these critical areas, examining how AI agents influence our social fabric, addressing the challenges of inequality and accessibility, and exploring the evolving landscape of policy and regulation.

Social and Cultural Impacts

Transforming Communication and Interaction

AI agents are revolutionizing the way we communicate and interact. From chatbots to virtual assistants, AI technologies are becoming integral to daily life, offering new modes of interaction and reshaping social norms.

Enhanced Communication

AI agents like Siri, Alexa, and Google Assistant have made information retrieval and task management more efficient, enabling people to perform tasks hands-free and access information quickly. These virtual assistants are not just tools but also companions for many, impacting how people interact with technology. For instance, voice assistants are increasingly used in smart homes to control appliances, set reminders, and even provide companionship for the elderly, thus altering daily routines and communication habits.

Moreover, AI-driven communication platforms such as chatbots are enhancing customer service by providing instant responses to queries. This has improved customer satisfaction and engagement across various sectors, including retail, banking, and healthcare. AI chatbots can handle multiple inquiries simultaneously, providing a level of efficiency and immediacy that human operators alone cannot match.

Social Media and Content Creation

AI-driven algorithms on social media platforms curate content tailored to individual preferences, enhancing user engagement. These algorithms analyze users' behavior and interactions to recommend content, connect people with similar interests, and even predict future preferences. This personalized content delivery keeps users engaged longer, but it also raises concerns about echo chambers and the reinforcement of biases.

Additionally, AI tools like DALL-E and GPT-4 enable the creation of content, from text to images, influencing media production and consumption. These tools can generate realistic images, write articles, create music, and even produce entire films. For instance, GPT-4 has been used to write news articles, blog posts, and even creative stories, while DALL-E can create intricate artwork from textual descriptions. This democratization of content creation allows more people to produce high-quality media without extensive technical skills, but it also challenges traditional notions of creativity and authorship.

Cultural Shifts

The integration of AI in daily life is driving cultural shifts. The acceptance of virtual influencers and AI-generated art is growing, challenging traditional notions of creativity and authorship. For instance, virtual influencers like Lil Miquela, an AI-generated character with millions of followers on social media, are becoming popular in marketing campaigns, influencing fashion trends, and shaping cultural conversations. These virtual personas interact with followers just like human influencers, blurring the lines between reality and artificiality.

AI-generated art and music are also gaining recognition and acceptance. AI systems like AIVA (Artificial Intelligence Virtual

Artist) compose music that has been performed by professional musicians, while AI-generated artworks have been sold at prestigious art auctions. These developments raise questions about the nature of creativity and the value of human versus machine-generated art.

Furthermore, AI is influencing language and communication styles. Predictive text and translation services are making communication more accessible across different languages and cultures. AI-powered tools like Google Translate have significantly improved in accuracy, enabling more effective cross-cultural communication and breaking down language barriers. However, this also leads to homogenization of language and potential loss of linguistic diversity.

Impact on Employment and Workforce Dynamics

The rise of AI agents is reshaping the employment landscape, bringing both opportunities and challenges.

Job Displacement and Creation

While AI automates routine tasks, potentially displacing certain jobs, it also creates new opportunities in AI development, maintenance, and oversight. For example, roles such as AI trainers, data scientists, and ethics officers are becoming increasingly important. According to a report by the World Economic Forum, by 2025, automation and AI could displace 85 million jobs globally, but they could also create 97 million new roles. These new roles will require a blend of technical and soft skills, emphasizing the need for workforce reskilling and upskilling.

Workplace Transformation

AI is transforming workplace dynamics by enabling remote work, enhancing productivity through automation, and fostering new forms of collaboration. Tools like AI-powered project management software and virtual meeting assistants are streamlining workflows and improving efficiency. For example, AI-driven tools can automate meeting scheduling, transcribe meeting notes, and provide actionable insights from discussions, allowing teams to focus on strategic tasks.

The COVID-19 pandemic accelerated the adoption of remote work, and AI technologies have played a crucial role in this transition. AI-powered tools for virtual collaboration, such as Zoom's AI background noise suppression and real-time transcription, have made remote work more productive and seamless. This shift is likely to have long-term implications, with many organizations adopting hybrid work models that combine remote and in-office work.

Skill Requirements

The evolving job market requires a shift in skill sets. There is a growing demand for technical skills such as programming and data analysis, as well as soft skills like critical thinking and adaptability. Lifelong learning and continuous skill development are becoming essential for career resilience. Educational institutions and employers are increasingly emphasizing STEM (Science, Technology, Engineering, and Mathematics) education and offering training programs to help workers adapt to the changing job landscape.

In addition to technical skills, human skills such as creativity, empathy, and emotional intelligence will be crucial for roles that require complex problem-solving and interpersonal interactions. For example, while AI can assist in diagnosing medical conditions, human doctors will still be needed to provide compassionate care and make nuanced decisions based on patient interactions.

Ethical and Psychological Considerations

The integration of AI agents into society raises important ethical and psychological questions.

Privacy Concerns

AI systems often require access to vast amounts of personal data, raising concerns about privacy and data security. The misuse of personal information by AI agents can lead to identity theft, discrimination, and other harms. Ensuring data privacy and security is paramount to gaining public trust in AI technologies. Regulations like the General Data Protection Regulation (GDPR) in Europe set important standards for data protection, but global cooperation and stricter enforcement are needed to address privacy concerns effectively.

Bias and Fairness

AI systems can perpetuate and amplify existing biases present in the data they are trained on. Ensuring fairness and eliminating bias in AI algorithms is a critical challenge that requires ongoing attention and mitigation strategies. For example, facial recognition technologies have been found to exhibit racial and gender biases, leading to wrongful identifications and discriminatory practices. Researchers and developers are working on techniques such as algorithmic fairness, diverse training datasets, and bias detection tools to address these issues.

Human-AI Interaction

The increasing reliance on AI agents can impact human psychology and behavior. The human tendency to anthropomorphize AI agents can lead to over-reliance on these systems, affecting decision-making processes and interpersonal relationships. For instance, people may develop emotional attachments to AI companions, which can impact their social interactions and mental well-being. It is important to maintain a balance between leveraging AI's capabilities and fostering meaningful human connections.

Moreover, the rise of AI in the workplace can lead to job-related stress and anxiety, particularly if employees feel their roles are threatened by automation. Organizations need to manage these transitions carefully, providing support and training to help employees adapt to new technologies and work environments.

Addressing Inequality and Accessibility

Bridging the Digital Divide

AI has the potential to bridge the digital divide, providing access to information and services to underserved communities. However, it also has the potential to exacerbate existing inequalities if not implemented thoughtfully.

1. **Access to Technology**: Ensuring equitable access to AI technologies is crucial. This includes providing affordable devices, internet connectivity, and digital literacy training to marginalized communities.
2. **Educational Opportunities**: AI can enhance educational opportunities through personalized learning platforms and online courses. However, it is essential to ensure that these resources are accessible to all students, regardless of their socio-economic background.

Inclusive AI Design

Designing AI systems that are inclusive and accessible to all individuals, including those with disabilities, is vital for creating an equitable society.

1. **Accessibility Features**: AI can improve accessibility through features such as speech-to-text, text-to-speech, and image recognition technologies. For example, AI-driven apps can assist visually impaired individuals by describing their surroundings or reading text aloud.
2. **Inclusive Development**: Involving diverse populations in the AI development process can help ensure that AI systems address the needs of all users. This includes considering different cultural, linguistic, and socio-economic contexts in the design and deployment of AI technologies.

Economic Disparities

Addressing economic disparities through AI requires targeted interventions and policies.

1. **Job Training and Reskilling**: Governments and organizations must invest in job training and reskilling programs to help workers transition to new roles created by AI advancements. This includes providing support for workers displaced by automation.
2. **Equitable Distribution of AI Benefits**: Ensuring that the economic benefits of AI are distributed equitably is critical. This may involve implementing policies that support small and medium-sized enterprises (SMEs) in adopting AI technologies and preventing the monopolization of AI resources by large corporations.

Policy and Regulation

Establishing Ethical Guidelines

Developing ethical guidelines for AI is essential to ensure that these technologies are used responsibly and for the benefit of society.

1. **AI Ethics Frameworks**: Various organizations and governments are developing AI ethics frameworks to guide the development and deployment of AI technologies. These frameworks address issues such as transparency, accountability, and fairness.
2. **Public Involvement**: Engaging the public in discussions about AI ethics can help build trust and ensure that AI technologies align with societal values. Public consultations and forums can provide valuable insights into the ethical considerations of AI.

Regulatory Measures

Implementing regulatory measures to oversee AI development and deployment is crucial to prevent misuse and protect public interests.

1. **Data Protection Laws**: Strengthening data protection laws can safeguard individuals' privacy and ensure that personal data is handled responsibly by AI systems. Regulations such as the General Data Protection Regulation (GDPR) in Europe set important precedents for data privacy. These laws mandate strict guidelines on data collection, processing, and storage, ensuring that individuals have control over their personal information and that organizations are held accountable for data breaches.
2. **AI-Specific Regulations**: Developing AI-specific regulations can address the unique challenges posed by AI technologies. This includes establishing standards for AI transparency, safety, and accountability. For example, requiring companies to disclose how their AI systems make decisions can help demystify AI processes

and build public trust. Additionally, setting safety standards for AI in critical applications, such as autonomous vehicles and healthcare, can prevent harm and ensure the reliability of these systems.

3.   **Ethical Use of AI**: Enforcing ethical guidelines in AI development can prevent the exploitation of AI technologies for malicious purposes. This involves regulating the use of AI in surveillance, ensuring that AI is not used to infringe on civil liberties, and promoting the development of AI systems that prioritize human well-being. For example, banning the use of AI for mass surveillance without proper oversight can protect individual freedoms.

International Cooperation

AI's global impact necessitates international cooperation and coordination.

1.   **Global Standards**: Establishing global standards for AI can ensure consistency and interoperability across different jurisdictions. International organizations such as the United Nations and the Organisation for Economic Co-operation and Development (OECD) play a key role in facilitating these efforts. These standards can cover various aspects of AI, including ethics, safety, data privacy, and cross-border data flows, ensuring that AI development aligns with shared global values.

2.   **Cross-Border Collaboration**: Promoting cross-border collaboration on AI research and development can drive innovation and address global challenges. Collaborative initiatives can leverage diverse perspectives and expertise to create AI solutions that benefit humanity. For instance, international research projects on AI for healthcare can pool resources and knowledge to develop advanced medical AI applications that improve global health outcomes.

Public Engagement and Education

Engaging the public in discussions about AI and educating them about its benefits and risks are crucial for fostering a well-informed society.

1. **Public Consultations**: Conducting public consultations on AI-related policies can ensure that diverse viewpoints are considered in the regulatory process. This can involve holding public forums, surveys, and discussions to gather input from various stakeholders, including industry experts, civil society organizations, and the general public.
2. **Educational Campaigns**: Launching educational campaigns to inform the public about AI technologies, their potential impacts, and ways to navigate the AI-driven world can empower individuals to make informed decisions. These campaigns can include workshops, online courses, and informational materials that explain AI concepts in accessible language.
3. **Transparency Initiatives**: Promoting transparency in AI development and deployment can build public trust. This includes requiring companies to disclose their AI policies, the datasets used to train AI systems, and the potential risks associated with AI applications. Transparent practices can help demystify AI technologies and reassure the public that AI is being used responsibly.

Summary

AI agents are poised to have profound social and cultural impacts, offering both opportunities and challenges. They are transforming communication and interaction, reshaping employment and workforce dynamics, and raising important ethical and psychological considerations. Addressing these impacts thoughtfully and proactively is essential to harness the benefits of AI while mitigating its risks and ensuring that these technologies contribute positively to society. Furthermore, implementing robust regulatory measures, fostering international cooperation, and engaging the public are crucial steps in creating an AI-driven world that aligns with societal values and priorities. By addressing issues of inequality and accessibility, and establishing clear ethical guidelines, we can ensure that AI agents serve as a force for good, promoting progress and well-being for all.

Chapter 18: The Future of AI Agents

The AI and tech industries are evolving at an unprecedented pace. What we see today as cutting-edge technology might be surpassed tomorrow by even more advanced innovations. This book has provided a comprehensive overview of AI agents, covering their development, capabilities, applications, and potential. However, given the rapid advancements in AI and technology, this book captures only a snapshot of the current state of AI agents. The future holds even more remarkable developments, which we must be prepared to understand and integrate into our lives and businesses.

Emerging Trends and Technologies

1. Advanced Personalization

One of the most promising trends in AI agents is the move toward advanced personalization. Future AI agents will utilize more sophisticated algorithms to create highly personalized experiences across various sectors, including healthcare, education, and entertainment. In healthcare, AI agents could offer individualized health monitoring, tailored treatment plans, and predictive diagnostics based on genetic profiles and lifestyle data. In education, AI tutors will adapt to students' learning styles and paces, providing customized lessons and real-time feedback.

2. Enhanced Natural Language Understanding

Natural Language Processing (NLP) is advancing, and future improvements will enable AI agents to understand and interact with human language more naturally and intuitively. This includes better context recognition, emotional intelligence, and nuanced understanding of human communication. These advancements will make AI agents more effective in customer service, virtual assistance, and mental health support, allowing for more empathetic and human-like interactions.

3. Integration with Augmented Reality (AR) and Virtual Reality (VR)

The convergence of AI with AR and VR technologies will open new possibilities for immersive and interactive experiences. AI agents will serve as guides in virtual environments, providing real-time information and assistance in contexts such as virtual tourism, remote work, and gaming. In the workplace, AR and VR combined with AI will revolutionize training and collaboration, enabling employees to interact with digital twins of physical objects and environments.

4. Autonomous Decision-Making

As AI agents become more autonomous, they will make decisions with minimal human intervention. This capability will be crucial in areas like autonomous vehicles, smart cities, and industrial automation. AI agents will manage complex systems, optimize operations, and respond to real-time data to make informed decisions, enhancing efficiency and safety in various sectors.

Ethical and Social Implications

1. Ensuring Ethical AI Development

With the increasing power of AI comes significant responsibility. Ethical AI development is crucial to prevent misuse and ensure AI technologies benefit society. This includes addressing biases in AI algorithms, ensuring transparency in AI decision-making, and protecting individuals' privacy and rights. Creating frameworks for accountability, where developers and organizations are held responsible for AI systems' actions, is essential, especially in high-stakes applications such as healthcare, law enforcement, and finance.

2. Addressing Workforce Displacement

The rise of AI agents raises concerns about workforce displacement. While AI creates new job opportunities, it also automates many tasks traditionally performed by humans. Addressing this challenge requires a proactive approach to workforce retraining and education. Governments, educational institutions, and businesses must collaborate to provide training programs that equip workers with the skills needed in an AI-driven economy.

3. Promoting Digital Inclusion

As AI becomes more integrated into daily life, ensuring digital inclusion is crucial. Everyone, regardless of socioeconomic status, should have access to AI technology benefits. This involves providing affordable access to digital devices, internet connectivity, and digital literacy programs. Efforts to promote digital inclusion should also focus on developing AI solutions that cater to diverse populations, including those with disabilities.

Preparing for an AI-Driven Future

1. Fostering Innovation and Research

Continued innovation and research are essential for advancing AI technology. Governments, academic institutions, and private companies must invest in AI research to explore new frontiers and solve existing challenges. Collaborative research initiatives can accelerate progress by bringing together diverse perspectives and expertise. Open-source projects and public-private partnerships will play significant roles in driving innovation and making AI advancements accessible to a broader audience.

2. Building Robust AI Infrastructure

Developing a robust AI infrastructure is critical for supporting AI agents' deployment and scalability. This includes creating high-performance computing environments, advanced data storage solutions, and efficient data processing frameworks. Scalable AI infrastructure will enable organizations to deploy AI solutions on a large scale, addressing complex problems and serving larger populations.

3. Encouraging Public Engagement and Education

Public engagement and education are vital for fostering a society that understands and embraces AI technology. Educating the public about AI's capabilities, limitations, and implications can demystify the technology and build trust. Initiatives such as public lectures, workshops, and educational campaigns can help raise awareness about AI. Encouraging public participation in AI policy discussions and ethical debates can ensure that diverse perspectives are considered in decision-making processes.

4. Developing AI Governance Frameworks

Establishing governance frameworks for AI is crucial for managing the technology's impact on society. These frameworks should include regulations, standards, and guidelines to ensure AI systems' responsible development and use. AI governance frameworks must address issues such as data privacy, algorithmic transparency, and accountability. International cooperation and collaboration are essential for creating harmonized standards that promote the safe and ethical use of AI globally.

Embracing the AI Revolution

As we look ahead, it is clear that AI will continue to transform our world in profound ways. By understanding the trends, addressing the ethical and social implications, and preparing for an AI-driven future, we can harness the power of AI agents to create a better, more equitable, and innovative society.

This book aims to provide a comprehensive guide to AI agents, covering their development, capabilities, applications, and future potential. As you embark on your journey into the world of AI, remember that the key to success lies in continuous learning, ethical responsibility, and a commitment to leveraging AI for the greater good. The future is AI-driven, and with the right tools and understanding, you can be at the forefront of this transformative era.

Made in the USA
Middletown, DE
29 September 2024

61672647R00166